Preaching God's Compassion

"Aden and Hughes have blended two perennial realities, proclamation and pastoral care, into a thoughtful volume on the church's public responses to suffering. Speaking from their years as seminary teachers and colleagues, this work realistically addresses suffering and Christian responses to it through the matrix of proclamation, theology, and the resources of pastoral care. In the current uneasy contexts of today's faith communities, this volume offers plenteous resources."

SUSAN K. HEDAHL
GETTYSBURG LUTHERAN THEOLOGICAL SEMINARY

"While recognizing the good intentions of its twentieth-century advocates, Aden and Hughes are convinced that pastoral preaching needs better conceptualization leading to more effectively faithful preaching. To this end, they emphasize the pastoral function of preaching, which establishes the sermon's formal movements, determines its teaching moments, and identifies the appropriate faith response to an instance of intractable or inescapable human suffering. . . . For pastors who know that what is most deeply personal is also most widely shared, but have longed for expert guidance in how to incorporate this insight into the public act of preaching, this engaging book will be an indispensable resource."

DONALD CAPPS
PRINCETON THEOLOGICAL SEMINARY

"The great strength of this welcome book emerges in chapters 5 through 9 where the authors engage those realities of suffering about which they have long thought deeply and in the practice of which they are richly experienced. The same care they bring to the distinction (but not separation) of pastoral care and pastoral preaching, they bring to the nuances of sorrow that stem from different causes. . . . All this, the more clearly to allow God's good news to address those of us in dire need."

SARAH S. HENRICH
LUTHER SEMINARY

Other Titles in
Fortress Resources for Preaching

Preaching as Local Theology and Folk Art
Leonora Tubbs Tisdale

Preaching Liberation
James H. Harris

Preaching Doctrine
Robert G. Hughes and Robert Kysar

Preaching Mark
Bonnie Bowman Thurston

Preaching John
Robert Kysar

Preaching God's Compassion
LeRoy H. Aden and Robert G. Hughes

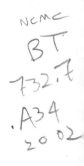
Preaching God's Compassion

Comforting Those Who Suffer

LeRoy H. Aden

Robert G. Hughes

Fortress Press
Minneapolis

PREACHING GOD'S COMPASSION
Comforting Those Who Suffer

Library of Congress Cataloging-in-Publication Data
Aden, LeRoy.
    Preaching God's compassion : comforting those who suffer / LeRoy H.
    Aden, Robert G. Hughes.
    p. cm.—(Fortress resources for preaching)
    Includes bibliographical references and index.
    ISBN 0-8006-3577-9 (alk. paper)
    1. Suffering—Religious aspects—Christianity—Sermons. 2. Sermons. English.
I. Hughes, Robert G. II. Title. III. Fortress resources for preaching

BT732.7 .A34 2002
251'.56—dc21   2002072556

Manufactured in the U.S.A.

07   06   05   04   03   02   1   2   3   4   5   6   7   8   9   10

To Our Wives

Ruth and Dona Lee

whose companionship along the way

has been an expression of God's compassion

∾

Contents

Preface

THIS BOOK IS ABOUT HUMAN SUFFERING. It is also about the church's attempt to minister to those who are suffering. While the book uses the resources of contemporary pastoral care to understand situations of suffering, it focuses mostly on pastoral preaching as the church's primary address to those who suffer.

We define pastoral preaching as the oral proclamation of God's Word from the perspective of caring for or comforting people in need. We will extend this definition in a later discussion, but for now it points to a minister's attempt from the pulpit to bring to parishioners who have particular needs a comforting and helpful word from God.

We recognize that human suffering comes in many different forms, both physical and emotional. To make our discussion manageable, we will narrow our consideration of suffering to five major types (see summary below). We also know that there are many different degrees of suffering, ranging from the mild upset of "feeling blue" to the traumatizing devastation experienced by Job in the Old Testament. Our discussion assumes a degree of suffering that prompts the individual to long for and seek some kind of relief.

Many books on suffering and on pastoral preaching have been published, but few combine them into a single concern. Helpful books in the field of pastoral care appear from time to time, covering topics like loneliness, guilt, grief, anger, and conflict, but rarely do they give guidance for biblically and theologically responsible preaching. On the preaching side, various sermonic publications offer a potpourri of exegesis, stories, and illustrations related to texts in the three-year lectionary, but only occasionally do such publications identify and provide help in addressing the pastoral issues that are implicit in the lectionary texts. A theoretical book of considerable value is J. Randal Nichols, *The Restoring Word: Preaching as Pastoral Communication.*[1] Lloyd M. Perry's and Charles M. Sell's *Speaking to Life's Problems: A Sourcebook for Preaching and Teaching* attempts to do what we propose, but it is now a dated book.[2] Also, because it was written in the evangelical revival tradition, it is of limited value to mainline preachers. In *Pastoral Counseling and Preaching: A Quest for an Integrated Ministry,* Donald Capps takes a structural approach to the relation between preaching and pastoral counseling and ends up making a significant contribution to pastoral preaching.[3] We use each of these resources as we develop our own thought.

The authors of the present book have been colleagues at the Lutheran Theological Seminary in Philadelphia for more than twenty-five years and have team-taught courses that benefit from the integration of pastoral care and preaching on at least five different occasions. Specifically, LeRoy Aden has coedited four books in the area of pastoral care and, in addition to many journal articles, has contributed to three dictionaries related to pastoral care and pastoral theology. Robert Hughes's first book, *A Trumpet in Darkness: Preaching to Mourners,* grew out of his doctoral studies and out of our team-taught courses. Published by Fortress Press in 1985, it has been reprinted twice, most recently in 1997 by Sigler Press. Hughes has also authored with Robert Kysar *Preaching Doctrine for the Twenty-First Century.*[4]

In the present work, we seek to be of help to seminary students and clergy of all denominations who are engaged in preaching, teaching, and caring. We think this book will be especially valuable to chaplains, but we also have in mind laypersons in local congregations who are members of discussion groups that meet to reflect on the life and faith of Christians.

We begin the book where many people in distress begin— reflecting on the reality of human suffering and examining the ways in which we try to make sense of it. When these explanations are not especially helpful, we turn to a Christian understanding of suffering. This understanding is more positive and comforting but by itself does not relieve us of the necessity to minister to those who suffer. On the contrary, it encourages us to take their suffering seriously and to minister to them in ways that mediate God's mercy and care.

We explore the pain of suffering in chapter 1. In chapter 2, we examine the believer's struggle with suffering. We describe three major questions the sufferer tends to put to God, then we return to reflect on each of the questions from the standpoint of preaching. We end the chapter by mentioning seven resources of the faith that are available to the suffering believer.

This brings us to chapter 3, where we take a historical look at the church's attempt to address suffering. Specifically, we center on what can be called pastoral preaching. We examine its historical antecedents, compare it with other forms of preaching, and arrive at a working understanding of the church's attempt to preach pastorally.

In chapter 4 we return to the pastor's response to suffering. Starting with the minister's pastoral relationship with troubled parishioners, we move toward the pastoral sermon by dealing with some of the practical differences that exist between pastoral counseling and preaching. We arrive at a functional approach to pastoral preaching, lifting out five of its major goals and illustrating the form of the pastoral sermon.

Chapters 5 through 9 are concerned with particular situations of suffering. We use the five types of suffering that Erhard S. Gerstenberger and Wolfgang Schrage find in the biblical witness, especially in the Old Testament.[5] We deal, in turn, with loss, illness, violence, fear, and failure and in each case suggest ways in which the pastor can preach to parishioners who are experiencing one or more of these traumas.

Finally, in chapter 10, we offer three different and provocative examples of how two preachers have attempted to preach pastorally. These examples do not represent absolute forms to be replicated; instead, their purpose is to encourage readers to examine and refine their own pastoral address.

∽

The authors have enjoyed a prolonged tenure of teaching at the Lutheran Theological Seminary in Philadelphia. It was in the crucible of that tenure that this book was fashioned. The seminary encouraged team-taught courses, and the authors used such courses as an opportunity to explore the mutual enrichment that can result when pastoral care and preaching enter into dialogue with each other. The seminary's generous sabbatical policy of funding regular sabbatical leaves for its tenured professors gave each of us the freedom to pursue studies that contributed to this book. Aden's retirement as Luther D. Reed Professor of Pastoral Theology and Hughes's return to his post as St. John Professor of Homiletics following nine years as president of the seminary made it possible to devote extended hours to this project. Both of us have been enlivened by our work together and have enjoyed laboring on the creative boundaries of our respective disciplines.

A grant from the Lutheran Brotherhood fraternal organization helped support Hughes's research. Spirit in the Desert, a Lutheran retreat center in Care Free, Arizona, provided a fruitful place for reflection and writing. The bishop and the pastors of the Grand Canyon Synod also need to be thanked. They appointed Hughes as "theologian in residence," and by their active participation in workshops and retreats, they contributed to the formation of the book.

The students in our team-taught courses contributed more than they will ever realize. Their earnest attempts to try their hand at pastoral preaching, whether successful or not, provided the authors with a forum in which the parameters of pastoral preaching became clearer.

Finally, we must acknowledge the pastors of the churches who, being on the front line week after week, have the daunting task of proclaiming God's compassion to people who are deafened by the clamor of suffering. Hughes, who as homiletics professor is often called upon to preach to a variety of situations, knows how demanding pastoral preaching can be. Aden, who often sits in the pew on Sunday mornings, knows how vital pastoral preaching is to those who are in need. Our hope is that this volume will honor the pastors who preach weekly and that it will support and enrich their ministries.

1

The Pain of Suffering

A FIFTY-YEAR-OLD SCHOOL TEACHER LOSES HER HUSBAND when he joins a cross-country bicycle trip through a southwestern state and is hit by an automobile driver who may have been playing "chicken" with the cyclists.

A college student dreams of being accepted into medical school only to discover once he begins the study of medicine that he is not going to make it.

A devoted mother of three young children is stopped short by the news that her chronic fatigue is caused by an untreatable form of cancer.

In each of these instances, the person is involved in suffering, a state of intense pain and distress. This is not unusual, for to be human is to be acquainted with suffering. The Book of Job is descriptive of our plight, perhaps not in terms of its intensity, but certainly in terms of its reality.

Job is a man of faith and also a man of immense wealth, one of "the greatest of all the people of the east" (Job 1:3). Satan comes before God and casts doubt on Job's faith: "Does Job fear God for nothing? Have you not put a fence around him? . . . You have blessed the work of his hands" (vv. 9-10). Satan predicts that if Job is made to suffer, his faith will be shaken, if not negated. God agrees to put Job to the test, and in turn Job is stripped of his possessions, his children, and his health. In a word, Job is immersed in intense suffering.

Our lives need not duplicate the plight of Job for us to know the magnitude of suffering. Suffering is all around us, and maybe we ourselves have experienced a good measure of it. If so, we know the pain of suffering and the dark shadow that it can cast on our lives.

And like Job we need someone to be with us in our distress, maybe even someone to help us find an answer to our misery.

The pain of suffering is often intense enough to drive us to do something about it. Douglas John Hall describes one of our most frequent reactions. Instead of acknowledging the suffering and tolerating the pain, we simply deny that we are suffering. Examples are abundant. The wife of an abusive husband covers up her hurt by saying that his actions are a justified response to her failures. The husband of an alcoholic lives for years with the hope that his wife will come to her senses and stop drinking. A child who is maligned and degraded by peers fabricates a world in which there is concord and recognition.

The denial of suffering or, as Hall describes it, the incapacity to suffer, is not only a personal response but also a societal prescription. We Americans are taught to believe that suffering can and will be overcome by "human ingenuity and inventiveness."[1] We buy into the American dream that diminishes the reality of human suffering, and then we, like Willy Loman in Arthur Miller's *The Death of a Salesman*, become pathetic creatures not because we suffer but because we "cannot face it."

Part of the pathos of our denial is its consequences. As Hall indicates, to deny suffering is to be subject to its impotencies: we cannot accept or articulate our own suffering, we cannot "enter imaginatively into the suffering of others,"[2] and we cannot acknowledge how we are often the cause of our own suffering. In other words, we are at the mercy of suffering, and there is no road out of it.

As we will see, that is part of the task of pastoral preaching—to give us the courage to face our own suffering. In the meantime, there is enough conscious suffering around to keep us busy. We are surrounded by parishioners who are aware of their suffering and who long to gain some relief from its pain. To the extent that they look to the church for this relief, we are challenged to preach pastorally to their needs.

The Misunderstanding of Suffering

Suffering is an interpreted fact, and how we see it either increases or decreases its effect on us. As Christians, we often see suffering in terms of God's relation to us. We can feel that God is either against us or for us. The first option is a common, almost a logical, perception, but it has major flaws. The second option requires a leap of faith, but it is more in line with our Christian theology. We will start with the first option and outline the three major forms suffering takes.

First, suffering can be seen as a punishment from God. This is the most common understanding of suffering, even in the Old Testament. In this understanding, suffering becomes a punitive act of God, the reaction of a just and angry God to our wicked and rebellious ways. The thought is usually taken to its logical end: God rewards the righteous and punishes the wicked. According to this principle, the righteous should enjoy health, peace, and prosperity while the sinful should suffer and be driven to despair.[3] The assumption that God rewards the righteous and punishes the wicked can be found in many places in the Old Testament. Psalm 1:3-4 says righteous people "are like trees planted by streams of water, which yield their fruit in its season, and their leaves do not wither. In all that they do, they prosper. The wicked are not so, but are like chaff that the wind drives away." And Psalm 37:9-10 says, "The wicked shall be cut off, but those who wait for the LORD shall inherit the land. Yet a little while, and the wicked will be no more." Job's three friends also believe that the wicked will be punished. They argue almost in the form of a neat syllogism: "Major premise: Since God is just, he always punishes sin with suffering. Minor premise: Job is undergoing great suffering. Inescapable conclusion: Job is a great sinner."[4]

In our day, Rabbi Harold Kushner, whose son Aaron died from progeria, believed initially in a God of retribution, a God of rewards and punishments. That is why when he first heard of his son's condition, he struggled with the question, "Why do the righteous suffer?" or, as he put it, I have tried "to do what [is] right in the sight of God. ... How could He do this to me?"[5] After much struggle, Kushner gave up the idea that God gives people what they deserve, that "our misdeeds cause our misfortune." He realized that this understanding of suffering has a "number of serious limitations. ... It teaches people to blame themselves. It creates guilt even where there is no basis for guilt. It makes people hate God, even as it makes them hate themselves. And most disturbing of all, it does not even fit the facts."[6]

Kushner is right. Our experience does not confirm the retribution theory. On the contrary, we often find that the wicked prosper while the righteous suffer. Actually, the retribution theory of suffering deserves a more detailed consideration. On the positive side, it rests on the conviction that God is a just God, that there is an eminent fairness in what God does, whether or not we can see it. It also rests on the conviction that God is sovereign, that there is nothing more powerful or in control than the Creator. Finally, it addresses our psychological need for punishment. It means that we are not burdened by unrequited guilt but that suffering comes as a just payment for our misdeeds.

In the end, though, suffering often turns these positive affirmations on their head so they end up being negative assertions. For example, suffering, when it comes to people who are considered good, casts grave doubt on the justice and fairness of God. "If God is just, why isn't that scoundrel suffering rather than me?" Suffering can also raise serious questions about the sovereignty of God. "If God really is in charge, why does God allow this to happen to me?" And finally, if suffering is seen as punishment, it tends to make our suffering meritorious. Suffering becomes a self-earned expiation of guilt or at least a partial compensation for it.

There is thus serious difficulty with seeing suffering as a punishment sent from God. The difficulty is not just theological; it is also pastoral. Suffering seen as punishment tends to complicate rather than strengthen the sufferer's relationship with God. God is seen as an alien and punitive power who judges the sufferer and thus makes his or her suffering worse. God is decidedly on the wrong side of suffering, leaving the sufferer without any gracious shelter.

Second, suffering can be seen as a test of faith. It becomes a probationary act of God by which God tries to determine how much we are really made of or how much we are willing to trust him. Kushner cites God putting Abraham to the test by suggesting the sacrifice of Isaac.[7]

As we have seen, the story of Job begins with this picture of God. God allows afflictions to come to Job to determine if he is truly a "blameless and upright man who fears" the Lord (Job 1:8). In addition to Job, other sections of the Old Testament portray God as probationary. In Judges 2:22—3:6, God raises up a number of judges to save Israel from its enemies. Each time a judge dies, the nation goes back to its evil ways and forgets God. God gets angry and decides to use foreign nations to test Israel to see whether "they would take care to walk in the way of the LORD as their ancestors did" (2:22).

In the New Testament the element of testing occurs, but it is often placed within the context of a different understanding of suffering. Suffering is seen as a way to remind us of our fragility and dependence. It moves us beyond the comforts of this life to seek comfort in God. Within this understanding, suffering is also a test of our faith, but it mobilizes our "powers of resistance and steadfastness."[8]

It is interesting to note that suffering, like God's law, can drive us to depend on and to trust in God. But to see suffering as an intentionally induced test from God is to make God a player of games or, even worse, a tyrannical ruler who uses power to test the powerless.[9] The net effect is to imply that God makes us prove that we are worthy of God's care and concern. God's image is tarnished by this abrasive thought when God agrees to let Satan put Job's faith to the test. "Is God really that fickle and unfeeling as to play with a person's life?" But more important, the idea that God's love is conditional goes against the gospel, which affirms that God's care is constant and freely given. And the sufferer is again left without a gracious shelter and instead feels that he or she is on trial before a merciless judge.

Finally, suffering can be seen as a form of divine discipline. It becomes an educational act of God, a means of chastening us to make us better moral creatures or more faithful disciples.

Chastening is a frequent theme in the wisdom literature of the Old Testament. Psalm 94:12: "Happy are those whom you discipline, O LORD, and whom you teach out of your law." In Job it is chiefly Elihu (Job 32–37) who promotes the educational understanding of suffering: "God indeed does all these things, twice, three times, with mortals, to bring back their souls from the Pit, so that they may see the light of life" (33:29-30). In the New Testament the classic example of suffering as chastening is in the story of the prodigal son.

In our day, Kushner, under the weight of suffering, considers the idea that God, like a good parent, uses suffering to "cure us of our faults and make us better people."[10] He quickly dismisses the thought, however, because he concludes that suffering is designed not to help the sufferer but "to defend God." Besides, he observes that there is often very little connection between the fault that needs to be repaired and the suffering that is incurred. So the sufferer ends up confused if not totally turned off. In the end, then, suffering that is meant to chasten us often does not work. Instead of making us more obedient to God, it can make us more bitter and less trusting.

In summary, the belief that God is against us in and through suffering comes in different forms. To see suffering as a punishment, as a test of faith, or as a chastening of our character assumes that God stands apart from our suffering and maybe even uses it for God's own purposes. This understanding of suffering may provide temporary relief or resolve, but it does not provide long-term comfort or encouragement. It tends to defeat the very purpose it hopes to achieve, namely, to fortify us against suffering by relating (ascribing) it to God. It ends up casting doubt on God and intensifying the pain of suffering.

Pastoral preaching must address this situation. While recognizing the grain of experiential truth that is in each of these understandings of suffering, it must help people to move beyond them. In a nutshell, it must help the sufferer to see that in suffering God is for us and not against us.

A Christian Understanding of Suffering

To see God in the very midst of our suffering requires a leap of faith. It is not evident to the sufferer that God is anywhere around, let alone close at hand. On the contrary, God seems very distant or, if present, seems like an uncaring part of the problem. C. S. Lewis, when tortured by grief, went so far as to call God a "Cosmic Sadist."

Over against our experience, the Christian faith is bold enough— or foolish enough—to declare that God is with us in suffering. It maintains that God is a suffering God, one who was born into and became a part of our world of travail. What we are talking about is an extension of the incarnation, the belief that God in Christ enters into our history and is with us in the actualities of our situation. This is a startling statement. It asserts not only that God is with us in suffering but also that our suffering causes him to suffer. Suffering, then, becomes a sad and painful event for both God and us, which is to say that God is with us in suffering in a profound and personal way.

Martin Luther's theology of the cross expresses a similar thought. It maintains that God is revealed and known in the "disgrace, poverty, and death" of Christ.[11] This crucified God is not found in the works of the world or in the speculations of the philosopher but in the weakness and defeat of the cross. Hidden in suffering, God is known by the suffering endured.

God with us in suffering has several important implications for our struggle with suffering. First, it means that we can take our struggle seriously. God graced our afflictions by experiencing them, by taking them upon himself. We do not need to pretend that suffering is unreal or unimportant, for Christ's incarnation invites us to acknowledge our pain and to give full recognition to our defeat or loss.

Second, suffering is not God's will. God may know about our suffering (omniscience), and God may be present in it (omnipresence), but God is not the cause of it. The cause is often lodged in our own history. It represents the natural working out of consequences that accrue from either our finiteness or our sin, from either our creaturely vicissitudes or our separation from the Source of life. In other words, there are forces in the world or choices in life that land us where we do not want to go.

In the short run, of course, the one who suffers may draw comfort from the idea that his or her suffering is God's will. Suffering is hard to bear "if it is a ghastly mistake." It is even hard to bear if it is a consequence of our own finiteness or sin. We gain more comfort by believing that it is God's will not just because it gives us a logical explanation for our suffering but also because we find it easier to accept and to bear. Nevertheless, to pin our suffering on God is a distortion of God's relation to the world, and in the long run it may pose a serious threat to the believer's faith in a gracious and crucified God.

Third, despite our abandonment of God, we are not forsaken. God is faithful in the midst of our unfaithfulness. This truth may not be apparent to the one who suffers. In fact, the sufferer may feel abandoned by God, and yet when the suffering is lifted, he or she may come to feel that God was there all the while. Sometimes, of course, the sufferer gains this assurance even as he or she is struggling with suffering.

Fourth, God's role in suffering is not passive but active. God does not merely stand by but "consoles us in all our affliction, so that we may be able to console those who are in any affliction" (2 Cor. 1:4).

For Paul comfort is used in a twofold sense: Either God strengthens the person and enables him or her to go through the crisis or God rescues the person from the situation. In either case, God sustains the sufferer, not just as a temporary reprieve from the situation but as a continually empowering presence.

Fifth, with God on our side, suffering can be transformative— not redemptive but transformative. It can increase our faith, our reliance on God. We have touched on this point before. Suffering, seen in proper perspective, may drive us to God, not because we want to escape further punishment but because we see life from a different angle. We realize that we live in a fallen world and that in our brokenness we make decisions and get into situations where suffering is the consequence. In other words, we see that we are part of the problem and that we cannot get out of it by our own power. We are driven to God. We realize that we must put our trust in a power that stands above and is more powerful than the finiteness and the distortions of life. And when we go to God, to our surprise we find ourselves embraced by a suffering, caring presence.

Sixth, suffering in the name of Christ can edify, can build up the fellowship in a twofold sense. Suffering and being comforted equips us to console others with the "consolation with which we ourselves are consoled by God" (2 Cor. 1:4). Having experienced God's comfort, we can enter into the afflictions of others in a much more empathic way, and in this sense we build up the fellowship by re-presenting (offering) the comfort of Christ to our wounded neighbors. We also build up the fellowship, because our suffering has redemptive value for others, not because it is meritorious for them but because it serves as an inspiring example to them, especially if they are weak in the faith. Besides, we are doing in our own way what Christ has done for us, namely, bear the pain and suffering of others and thus lighten their load and take away their isolation. Paul says that he is "completing what is lacking in Christ's afflictions for the sake of his body, that is, the church" (Col. 1:24). By this phrase he does not mean that we complete, or add anything to, the saving work of Christ. Instead, he means that as Christians we are united with Christ in sufferings like his and that when we endure those sufferings for the sake of the church, we are carrying on his mission and work, that is, we are building up the fellowship.

However noble, the Christian understanding of suffering does not empower the sufferer to grasp onto it. Intellectually we may affirm the idea that God is with us in suffering, but under the actual weight of suffering we may find it very difficult to believe. We need the church's help, sometimes in every form that it can give. Our special concern, of course, is with the role of pastoral preaching in this process, but before we get to that we need to clarify what suffering requires of the pastor who seeks to address it.

Suffering and the Pastoral Task

After an extended consideration of God's role in Job's suffering, Dorothee Soelle declares, "Not the one who causes suffering but only the one who suffers can address Job."[12] In other words, anyone who would attempt to help the sufferer must be personally acquainted with suffering. Christ himself taught us this lesson. He did not stand above or apart from suffering but took it upon himself and not only identified with the sufferer but also identified God as a God who suffers.

The pastor who would help the sufferer must do the same thing. The pastor can properly and helpfully address suffering only if he or she stands alongside the sufferer. Anything less than this turns the sufferer off or may even increase his or her distress.

The need to stand with the sufferer in his or her suffering defines the basic task of pastoral ministry. Negatively, it means that suffering cannot be addressed by the mere repetition of doctrinal statements however true the statements may be. To say to the sufferer, "You know that God is with you in this ordeal" or even, "Remember! God knows how you feel, because he suffered the loss of his Son," is generally not helpful. Such platitudes come from a place outside of suffering that stands aloft from its reality and pain, and they give no indication that the pastor has been schooled in the ways of suffering. Paul has pastoral wisdom on his side when he observes that those who have been afflicted and have been consoled are equipped to console others who are afflicted, not with a comfort they devise but with a comfort they have received.

The point that we are trying to make finds expression in Carl Rogers's concept of empathic understanding.[13] Rogers maintains that in order for the therapist to be helpful to the troubled client, the therapist must lay aside his or her preoccupations and enter imaginatively into the world of the client. The therapist must stand where the client stands, grasping the nuances of his or her world with understanding and precision. If the therapist succeeds in this endeavor, he or she is able to speak from inside the person's distress and give authentic expression to the client's troubled life.

Rogers maintains that "being with" the client has healing effects, partly because it helps the client to understand what is really happening in his or her world and partly because it means that the client is not alone, that in fact a supportive person stands alongside. According to Rogers, this "being with" awakens resources within the client and allows the client to pursue an authentic form of his or her existence.

While we find Rogers's concept of empathic understanding helpful in terms of the need to stand with the sufferer, we think that his idea that it heals by releasing inner resources is not the whole truth. We think it heals because it incarnates the empathic suffering of God in a live human relationship. The good news of God, that is, that God is with us and is present to us in suffering, becomes a concrete reality and as such becomes a blessed assurance against the agony and loneliness of suffering. If God is seen as being on our side, our suffering may not disappear, but its implied judgment and its very real pain are diminished by being cast in a more hopeful light.

Once the importance of ministering to the sufferer by standing with the person is established, the question becomes, "How does ministry incarnate the suffering of Christ?" or, more personally, "How do we make real the living presence of Christ in the sufferer's world?" The task is not easy. It can be accomplished at best only in degrees, and yet it is imperative to our ministry to deal with the question of how.

Pastoral counseling may achieve this incarnation easier than other forms of ministry. It has emphasized the need to get into the parishioner's frame of reference and thus to concretize help not by bringing an alien word to the sufferer but by standing with the sufferer. Successful pastoral counseling has its noticeable limits in that it tends to address only one individual at a time. Besides, it has sometimes acted as though empathic understanding is sufficient unto itself, that it can bring comfort and strength on its own merits. On the contrary, we see empathic understanding as a means to a more transcendent end. We think it should serve as a medium through which God's suffering presence is communicated and actualized to the person who is walking in a dark valley.

Pastoral preaching is another form of ministry that is concerned about the sufferer. It too seeks to incarnate the incarnation of Christ and to bring the suffering Christ into the sufferer's world. As we see it, that is its basic task, but how it accomplishes that task is often not apparent. That is why the act of pastoral preaching is our primary concern in this book. We will not come out with any neat or sure formulas, but we hope to clarify the nature of pastoral preaching and to indicate how it can be made more effective as a conduit of God's comfort. We begin our inquiry by taking a close look at the believer's struggle with suffering and how it might be addressed.

2

The Believer's Struggle
with Suffering

CHRISTIANS ARE NOT IMMUNE TO SUFFERING, as indicated in chapter 1. The people of God have struggled with suffering since the Old and New Testaments and have formulated certain understandings of suffering to try to make some sense of it in light of God's relation to the world. These formulations have not put an end to all questions. In some cases, they have actually led to more serious questions, often about the very nature of life and God.

Today Christians who suffer often find themselves in the same situation. After all, suffering and its concomitant emotions evoke intellectual distress in believers and cause a state of disequilibrium. Christians who have experienced violence, illness, or loss often describe themselves as "confused," "off balance," or "being knocked for a loop." This state of affairs may last for a sustained period of time, whether we are talking about individuals, small groups, or an entire congregation.

Persons in a state of disequilibrium try to regain some sense of balance. They thrash about, grasping for support and trying to keep from collapsing. Sometimes they deny that there is a problem, or they put the blame on some external authority. For believers, God may become the scapegoat or, at the very least, God may be the target of three agonizing questions. We need to deal with these questions head-on, because they are a vital and central concern to pastoral preaching.

The Struggle with God

"Oh God, Why?"

"Why?" is a universal question writ bold across the face of suffering. The drive to know, the compulsion to make sense of suffering evokes the question. Because suffering frequently seems irrational and meaningless, it demands an explanation, it lingers on the lips of the sufferer as an angry or confused "Why?"

Sometimes pastors are asked the question directly by troubled parishioners, but more often the question is an expletive whispered only in the heart. People in distress may be too timid to ask an "ambassador of God" or too embarrassed by the intensity of their emotion, especially if it is fueled, as it often is, by anger. Whether the question is articulated or not, the struggle with why often masks the more personal and distressing question of "Why me?" We might expect to hear this question from someone who is critically ill or on the verge of death, but we quickly learn that the question can be spawned as well by sickness, pain, or disappointment, whether they are major incidents or not.

The logical endpoint of "Why me?" is "God, why are you doing this to me?" If God is all-powerful and is really in charge of the universe, why is God causing or allowing me to suffer? It is a question of justice. It is the age-old concern of why some people suffer while others do not. If I am the one who is suffering, the question takes on existential import. And I tend to identify more with Thornton Wilder's first thought than with his second thought: "Some say that . . . to the gods we are like the flies that the boys kill on a summer day; some say, on the contrary, that the very sparrows do not lose a feather that has not been brushed away by the finger of God."[1]

"God, What Did I Do to Deserve This?"

If we add a measure of self-righteousness to the why question, "Why are you doing this to me?" turns into "What did I do to deserve this?" The question may be asked in anger or in agony, but in either case it often comes out of a shallow view of sin. The sufferer assumes that he or she has earned more equitable treatment from God, that he or she has lived a life worthy of more consideration. In other words, the question is another way to ask about the justice of God. "Is God really treating me fairly, given my track record?"

If the sufferer focuses not on what he or she deserves but on what he or she has done or not done, guilt becomes an operative dynamic in the struggle with suffering. The person in distress assumes that God is making him or her pay a price for wrongdoing. This situation is often aggravated by our culture, which is quick to blame the individual for whatever appears to go wrong in life.

The Bible indicates that things done or left undone are only symptoms of a deeper malady that does indeed impact on human suffering. The depth dimension of sin and guilt is portrayed in Scripture in the repeated breaking of the faith relationship with God. Even the twelve disciples were guilty of failing to trust Jesus. James and John demanded special places in the kingdom. Peter denied the Lord while Judas betrayed him. A great deal of human suffering can be traced to our failure to trust in God and to give our lives back to God in obedience.

Sometimes feelings of guilt are linked not to a person's own suffering but rather to the suffering of a loved one. If a child is born retarded or disabled, parents frequently feel responsible. If a baby is not healthy, the mother may feel guilty even if prenatal care was adequate, and smoking and drinking were given up during pregnancy. If adult children divorce, parents may feel that, in some way, they have failed. In all of these situations, the sufferer is struggling with the question "What did I do to deserve this?" The individual presupposes that he or she is guilty and that the guilt has brought on the suffering.

"Oh God, Where Are You?"

Persons stricken with grief, pain, or injustice often feel abandoned. They feel that friends are not sufficiently attentive, or they may see that discomfort in the presence of suffering causes even loved ones to keep their distance.

> Nothing makes us feel as lonely as suffering does, whether it is physical or emotional. The loneliness is there even in the midst of family and friends. Even though they say, "I know how you feel," they do not. They cannot. They are not in your shoes. Your pain, your grief, your questions are unique.[2]

In the midst of suffering, God may also seem far removed, if not absent. God's apparent withdrawal is particularly painful to believers, for when they need God the most, they experience God as uncaring if not unavailable. As C. S. Lewis says, "Go to God when your need is desperate, when all other help is vain, and what do you find: A door slammed in your face, and a sound of bolting and double bolting on the inside. After that, silence. . . . Why is He so present a commander in our time of prosperity; and so very absent a help in time of trouble?"[3] As Lewis's comment implies, the absence of God is a consequence of our grief, but it also complicates our grief.

Persons whose grief turns into clinical depression frequently withdraw from the world both physically and emotionally. They become detached and self-absorbed. God's apparent absence becomes a reflection of the person's own withdrawal. Depressed persons may also experience a lethal combination of guilt and anger. They level blame against both the self and others, which only aggravates the apparent distance of friends, physicians, clergy, and even God. In an ultimate sense, they are wrestling with the question, "Where are you, God?" but in a relative sense, they are also experiencing distance and isolation in all their earthly relationships.

Family members, friends, and even caregivers may rush in with hurried reassurance. "Snap out of it! Of course God hears your prayers." Cutting off the expression of aloneness will tend to drive the distressed person further into silence and short-circuit the healing process.

Pastors and chaplains should not assume that expressions of God's absence, that even angry accusations of abandonment, necessarily signal the loss of faith. On the contrary, while trust in God may indeed wane in the face of torment, cries of absence may signal a deepening need for God.

> The experience of God's absence is painful to those who struggle to experience the living Word of God. The more precious that Word the more acutely its absence will be felt. To the unbeliever, God's silence is normal. For the believer, the breakdown of communication is tragic.[4]

Preparing to Preach

When suffering induces a struggle with God, the pastor is, at least potentially, a pivotal resource. In any case, the pastor must take the believer's struggle with suffering seriously, even before he or she gets into the pulpit. Each of the believer's questions deserve forethought, partly to clarify where the pastor is coming from as he or she addresses the questions and partly to anticipate some of the resources of the faith that are available to him or her. Before we turn to each question, however, it is important to identify a trap that pastors easily can fall into as they attempt to address those who suffer.

The pastor must avoid what we call the trap of magical thinking. As he or she faces a desperately ill parishioner or recalls a church leader who is going through a nasty divorce or remembers a grieving widow who is obviously distraught, he or she may be tempted to suggest that God will take away the hurt. The temptation may come out of a sincere desire to help, or it may be a response to the pastor's own sense of helplessness in the face of suffering, but in either case it is neither helpful nor appropriate.

Well-intentioned preachers foster magical thinking in listeners when they portray God as a heavenly superhero who intervenes at a moment's notice to eliminate distress. They may convey the same message when they infer that God's love is an instant help that takes away all the hurt. A mother's kiss may make the bruise feel better, but it does not produce instant healing. It is better to be more modest—and more realistic—in our claims. Our faith assures us that God is active in our broken world, seeking the best for God's creatures. This assurance can make a profound difference to believers in torment, but we should remain faithful to the biblical message that says that hope in Christ begins by acknowledging the reality of suffering. Israel experienced both the wilderness and the exile. The prophets were afflicted, and it is only by Jesus' "bruises [that] we are healed" (Isa. 53:5).

A second kind of magical thinking was identified and critiqued earlier, namely, the attempt of some preachers to turn life's negatives into positives. These preachers set out to find and to give answers to manageable human dilemmas. The answers may be satisfying to some people, or they may function as an anesthetic to dull pain. While we need to grant that positive thoughts and hopeful attitudes are preferable and more healthful than a gloomy demeanor, we also need to realize that easy answers become a sham in the face of intractable problems and profound distress.

We can now turn back to each of the three questions that sufferers put to God and offer preliminary thoughts on addressing them.

The Why Question

As pastors we need to remember that when parishioners express hostility toward God, or even when they raise serious questions about God's justice, we may become defensive. The temptation to defend God may be stifled in one-to-one or small-group situations, but homiletical literature abounds with evidence that pastors are tempted to use sermons to provide a sturdy defense of God's goodness and justice. God does not need our protection. Nor is God served well when preachers offer rational explanations for human suffering. Job was not comforted when his friends came with their cognitive conclusions. And the preacher who uses a sermon to explain God's reasons for suffering is not only inviting misunderstanding but also may be deepening the anger that evoked the why question in the first place.

Scripture helps us to eliminate some of the false, or partially false, answers to the sufferer's "why." For example, the Old Testament affirms that premature and tragic death is contrary to God's will. Scripture is equally clear that suffering should not be viewed as a punishment for individual sins. Job's multiple tragedies, for example, were not retribution for particular shortcomings. In fact, the Lord says to Satan that Job is "a blameless and upright man who fears God and turns away from evil" (Job 1:8). In the New Testament, Jesus makes it clear that the eighteen people on whom the tower of Siloam fell and the worshiping Galileans who were slain by Pilate were not punished because they were worse sinners than other people (Luke 13:1-5). This is also true of the blind man whom Jesus healed. He was not born sightless because of his own particular sins or those of his parents (John 9:3).

These citations from Scripture do not mean that we know the mind of God in intimate detail. Paul reminds the Corinthians, who were claiming intimate knowledge of God, that our knowledge of the Lord's ways remains imperfect (1 Cor. 13:1-2). In a fallen world where the kingdom is inaugurated but not fully realized, God's action is concealed from us and is often misunderstood by us. The sight of believers is dim and partial at best (1 Cor. 13:12).

Preachers, then, need to take their partial sight seriously, even as they proclaim the comfort of God. Martin Luther, in the Heidelberg Disputation, gives us a proper approach to suffering. "He deserves to be called a theologian . . . who comprehends the visible and manifest things of God seen through suffering and the cross."[5] It is in the death of Jesus that God's heart of love is revealed. It is the sufferings of Christ, in his being misunderstood, rejected, and finally killed, that we are given life. We can boldly proclaim the good news of a God who is "appalled by human suffering and . . . [who] is trying to do something about it."[6]

We have no complete and final answer to the "why" of any particular instance of pain. But we do have an "Answerer," a God who in Christ entered the world to be with us in our suffering. If God did not abandon Jesus in his sufferings, God will not abandon us in ours. Our "Answerer" will be with us in all the dark places our lives may go. It is important for us to remember that comfort as we seek to comfort others.

The What Question

As the parishioner deals with "What did I do to deserve this?" the initial role of the pastor-preacher is not to respond but to listen. Patient listening, the kind that encourages the sufferer to express both emotions (what sufferers feel) and questions (what sufferers are asking) will help to ensure that when a response is given it will be on target. Besides, careful listening helps to unearth a true understanding of the distress (what suffering means to the individual), ensuring that when the pastor-preacher speaks, he or she is addressing the real world of the sufferer.

In a society where few people seem ready to accept responsibility for their actions, a measure of guilt may be healthy. Guilt may be an appropriate response to deeds done or left undone, but the pastor-preacher has certain truths to bring to the situation. The lectionary-appointed or freely chosen lessons from Scripture give preachers the opportunity to deepen their listeners' understanding of sin. Sin is not primarily deeds done or left undone. It is a strained or broken relationship with God, putting everything else out of whack.

Redeemed and sinful believers need to learn and reappropriate this lesson throughout life.

Preaching can also help to correct the common misperception that sin is an individual problem located solely within the self. This individualizing of sin has effectively eliminated the corporate sense of sin and guilt. It has "reduced the scope of the gospel, slicing off the social shape of sin and scaling down the high and holy God of Israel to a salve for inner problems."[7] Most of us function as social beings, which means that we are motivated by class, racial, ethnic, or regional values and by ideological commitments. Sin is manifest when we try to preserve our social identities and promote them as absolute truths.

If "undeserved suffering" seems to be an issue with the sufferer, preachers need to clarify that God neither rewards good deeds nor punishes evil ones. Many New Testament passages seek to uncouple any presumed connection between individual or group wrongs and specific instances of suffering. The saying "They got what they deserved" is not descriptive of God's reaction to our suffering. God does not have a "tit-for-tat" approach to our predicaments but instead is there to extend comfort and forgiveness.

Sometimes guilt seems to be fed by a distorted sense of responsibility. Christians may feel, quite inappropriately, that they could or should have done something to prevent suffering. Often this ascribes more power or more control to the sufferer than he or she actually has. The good news of the gospel is that God is in charge, that we are freed from the anguish of needing to "play God" if we can "let God be God."

The Where Question

In a pastoral conversation, it is usually a mistake, psychologically and theologically, to reassure sufferers too quickly about God's presence in suffering. Hasty reassurance tends to discount an individual's experience of God's absence and may serve to increase guilt. At the same time, easy comfort may result in God's presence being taken for granted.

The experience of God's absence should be taken seriously in preaching. It is important to remember that congregations, and even large communities in distress, may share the feeling of being rejected by the very one in whom they trust. When a major industry closes, when a tragic explosion takes lives, when a shooting occurs at a local high school, the whole community shares a deep sorrow, and those who are religious may find themselves asking, "Where is God?" The anguish of suffering needs to be acknowledged in sermons before the good news of God's presence can be proclaimed or heard.

In the face of God's apparent absence, the pastor-preacher may counsel believers to wait patiently for God's voice to be heard again. Because sin persists in the lives of the redeemed, doubt and despair are painful but normal experiences. Waiting in hope indicates trust in the promises of God that the Word once spoken will be spoken again. Active waiting may take the form of prayer, asking God to break the silence (Matt. 7:7-11). Jesus' parable of the importunate widow and the judge counsels persistence in prayer.

Christ's own experience of abandonment will bring comfort to some people who are in distress. In Gethsemane, Jesus' disciples, though physically present, were sound asleep during the Lord's ordeal of being greatly "distressed and agitated" (Mark 14:32-42). And on the cross Jesus uttered the so-called cry of dereliction. Mark writes, "At three o'clock Jesus cried out with a loud voice, 'Eloi, Eloi, lema sabachthani?' which means, 'My God, my God, why have you forsaken me?' " (15:34). Because Jesus' identification with the Father was so close, the absence (rejection) of God must have been a devastating experience. Christians can draw comfort from Jesus' experience, for he was "despised and rejected by others; a man of suffering and acquainted with infirmity" (Isa. 53:3).

Of course, Jesus' death was not the last word. God's answer to the lynch mob was to raise Jesus from the dead. And the resurrection tells the people of God (the people of faith) that the cross was a victory over suffering, sin, and death. By "loosening the power of death," God forged a new relationship between himself and his people.

The preacher must help the people to see that Jesus' suffering and death are radically different from ours. Christ's death not only gives us the possibility of forgiveness but also reveals to us the reality of a suffering God. God is with us in our weakness, failure, and rejection. He suffers with us and makes it possible for us to die in the arms of God's love.

"Where is God?" God may seem distant to those who are in distress, but it is precisely through the experience of suffering that God becomes available to believers. God is found where God seems most absent, namely, in the moments when we feel abandoned by God and overwhelmed by suffering.

As a preparation for preaching, we have tried to clarify some of the issues or concerns that are involved in a believer's struggle with suffering. Now we must lay a firm foundation for the preacher to address the sufferer.

The Pastor's One Foundation

In chapter 1 we said that in order to address the sufferer the pastor-preacher must stand with the sufferer. No one who stands outside of suffering can address those who stand in it. That defines the basic pastoral task of the pastoral preacher.

Can the pastoral preacher achieve this by his or her own intuitive wisdom? While a little wisdom will certainly not hurt, it is not sufficient against the assaults of suffering. Only Christ, who himself is acquainted with suffering and who in the end was victorious over it, is able to address the sufferer.

The theology of the cross is all about a suffering Christ. It provides an orientation for clergy who seek to respond to human suffering through the magnitude of God's care and the proclamation of God's Word. The theology of the cross faces despair honestly while proclaiming the hope of the gospel. Consequently, it is the anchor for our pastoral preaching.

The cross of Christ was at the center of Paul's understanding of the gospel. While the apostle stressed a right relationship with God through faith in Christ in his Letter to the Romans, Paul made the cross itself the focal point in the Corinthian correspondence. He did this in order to proclaim a God of grace rather than a God of power. The Corinthian Christians believed that the cross had been occluded by Jesus' glorious resurrection, so Paul stressed that the resurrected one remains the crucified one.

Following Paul's lead, Martin Luther decided in terms of theological outlook "to know nothing among you except Jesus Christ, and him crucified" (1 Cor. 2:2). In the spring of 1518, Luther set forth a Pauline *theologia crucis* (theology of the cross) over against the reigning theology of the day, which he called a theology of glory. For Luther the theology of the cross was not one theological theme among others. Instead, the death and resurrection of Jesus was for him the lens through which the whole content of the faith should be seen.

A theology of the cross is decisive to pastors who seek to proclaim the gospel to suffering believers. The cross points to a suffering God in contrast to a theology of glory that lifts God above life's ills. God's power does not wield control over all day-to-day events, and thus events can occur that are counter to God's loving will. Christians can experience anger, guilt, and even abandonment as did Jesus. To the questions raised by suffering we have only partial and tentative answers. We see dimly and live with ambiguity. Thomas Long expresses this Christian realism in *The Witness of Preaching*:

> Whenever preaching presents human dilemmas and then says, "Here is how the gospel can speak to those problems," the inevitable conclusion is that the gospel is a finished and ready resource requiring only that we apply it to our circumstances. The truth is, the promised victory of God is not yet fully present or realized. Some tragic human suffering remains, for the time being, unintelligible and meaningless to us. Some conflicts are for the moment beyond resolution. Some illnesses have no available cure; some problems contain no ready answer.[8]

The theology of the cross seeks to link authentic hope to genuine honesty in the face of suffering. Because God is suffering love, sensitivity to distress resides in the heart of God. God suffers when we suffer. Violence, pain, fear, failure, and loss sadden God when they scar us. But beyond the pain, Christians experience God's presence in the midst of trouble. Douglas John Hall points to the theology of the cross as a seldom-tried tradition in Christian history that attempted "to proclaim the possibility of hope without shutting its eyes to the data of despair, a tradition which indeed insisted that authentic hope comes into view only in the midst of apparent hopelessness."[9]

A theology of a crucified and risen Lord challenges all other traditions that appear to compromise the radical message of the gospel, just as we will challenge any pastoral preacher who reduces the gospel to a theological pill for human ills. A theology centered in the cross chooses revelation over speculation, struggle in opposition to achievement and faith over sight. This theology affirms the paradoxical and troubling truth that faith sees best in the dark.

Resources for Pastoral Ministry

The theology of the cross provides pastors with resources to confront distress honestly while proclaiming the hope of the gospel. Some of the resources identified here are in addition to the comfort that pastoral preaching can provide; many of them, as we will see, are aspects of the faith that can be used in pastoral preaching itself. In any case, all of them serve as vital resources for the believer as he or she struggles with suffering.

The Word of God

Scripture and the preached word are direct means for God to engage those who are suffering. Half a century ago John Baillie wrote that "revelation is not merely *from* Subject to subject, but also *of* Subject to subject and what God reveals to us is Himself."[10] For Christians, Christ is the center and subject of revelation, the revealer and the revealed. He is the Word of God incarnate.

Scripture reading and preaching are not just words about Christ, not just talk about what new life can mean, but they are the means through which the crucified and risen Lord speaks to sufferers today. "Do not let your hearts be troubled. Believe in God, believe also in me" (John 14:1). Christ challenges those who suffer and are troubled to have faith in what he can do in us and for us. But we need to remind ourselves: The presence of Christ in the Word is at least partially hidden from our cloudy vision; consequently, we may not be able to see past the trouble of the moment. So faith becomes the act of trusting in his Word and his promises in spite of appearances.

Baptism

In Paul's writings baptism is proleptically the death of the Christian to sin (Rom. 6:2). Thus death as final judgment is dislodged, which means that physical suffering and death have lost much of their sting for those who believe.

Symbolically, baptismal fonts are graves, and the water is drowning. But fonts also signify wombs and cleansing. New life begins in the baptismal water (Rom. 6:4) as candidates are initiated into a fellowship where sin and death are overcome in daily repentance and forgiveness. In daily life believers may succumb to anxiety, self-assertion, and pride, but in the Spirit they already begin to experience new life.

In the minds of most worshipers, the significance of baptism is reduced to acceptance as a church member. If this misperception is not challenged by the pastor-preacher, baptism loses its power to witness to God's renewal of our tattered lives.

The Eucharist

With its tangible earthly elements, our manna in the wilderness of suffering, the Eucharist is reassurance that we have not been abandoned. This feast of suffering love looks back to Christ's own suffering and declares that we are partakers of his victory. The presence of Christ in the feast means that those who suffer participate in his resurrection. The one who died a death of pain and agony is alive, and through the meal of bread and wine, of his body and blood, we are not alone in our torment.

Furthermore, the meal is pregnant with eschatological promise. It proclaims "the Lord's death until he comes" (1 Cor. 11:26). It looks forward to the messianic banquet and the culmination of Jesus' reign. In the meantime, it draws us out of our isolation and gathers us at the table with fellow sufferers. Christ crucified by suffering and sin and raised by God is in our midst.

Discipleship

Discipleship is a daily dying and rising again as believers journey with Christ in the world under the guidance of the Holy Spirit. The Christian life is not being but becoming, not possession but progress, as we seek to "grow up . . . into Christ" (Eph. 4:15). Christians struggle to put their unconditional trust in Christ as they encounter the trials and tribulations of this life. And it is comforting to know that God does not abandon us when we, in our suffering, lose faith in God.

The call to discipleship is a journey of faith that also becomes active in love. The love of Christ poured into our hearts draws us in love toward our neighbor. Seeing the suffering of others, we seek to alleviate distress and to do justice, even as we ourselves are cradled in the arms of God's care in the midst of our suffering.

The Psalms

The psalms provide a language for human lament. Suffering, as we have noted, often reduces afflicted persons to silence. Our culture has few words and even less patience to enable us to express the deep pain of suffering.

The psalms provide forms for both private and corporate articulations of suffering. Where they are used in the liturgy, they function primarily as an unobtrusive transition from an Old Testament reading to a New Testament reading. Unfortunately, the psalms are rarely used in preaching, even though psalms like 23, 90, 118, and 130 are commonly used in funeral liturgies because they include both the reality of suffering and the sure hope of divine assistance. The use of psalms, especially in pastoral preaching, can give poetic expression to our suffering and manageable form to our grief. "How long, O LORD? . . . How long must I bear pain in my soul, and have sorrow in my heart all day long?" (Ps. 13:1-2).

Prayer

Prayer is a ready resource for believers in the face of life's negative happenings. In the midst of suffering, when God's countenance is hidden and prayer seems ineffectual, God insists on conversation. "Call on me in the day of trouble; I will deliver you, and you shall glorify me" (Ps. 50:15). "Pray without ceasing, give thanks in all circumstances; for this is the will of God in Christ Jesus for you" (1 Thess. 5:17-19). When we are angry with God, when we have no inclination to pray, the will of God summons us.

Believers who turn to God in prayer frequently find comfort. No specific words are required. The Spirit hears sighs too deep for words. A petition to God can be expressed anywhere at any time, though there are also collections of written prayers that give expression to our deepest feelings and questions. Within the worshiping community there is solace in the corporate prayers of the faithful. In that setting prayers of thanksgiving and intercession lift sufferers out of themselves, reopening both vertical and horizontal lines of communication.

Prayer is not simply a one-way conversation. God also addresses us in prayer, if we stop long enough to hear his still, small voice. This may be especially necessary when we are preoccupied with our suffering and are anxious to have God hear us.

The Fellowship of Christ

God's new humanity is coming to birth in the midst of a broken world. The promises of God are beginning to be fulfilled among us. The church, though broken itself, is "a sign of the new order in an old-order world" insofar as it is empowered by the Spirit.

Alongside the church, other communities and resources of healing bear witness to the new life of the gospel. In the film *28 Days,* Sandra Bullock plays the role of Gwen, a confused woman whose dependency on drugs and alcohol have caused her to be sentenced to a month in a rehabilitation facility. Gwen's major problem is her distorted conviction that she can make it on her own. "I can stop any time." Even after Gwen begins to face her addiction, she is inclined to go it alone. Finally, she is instructed to wear a sign reading, "Confront me ... if I don't ask for help." Asking and giving help, being supported by and supporting fellow sufferers, is at the heart of communities that bear the witness and the healing of the crucified Christ.

Conclusion

We have looked at the believer's struggle with suffering both as a struggle with God and as a prelude to our pastoral preaching. We have maintained that a theology of the cross, because it finds Jesus identifying with and standing alongside the sufferer, is the sure foundation from which our pastoral preaching should proceed. Finally, we delineated some of the resources that are available to our pastoral preaching, either as resources within the pastoral relationship or as themes in preaching itself. All of these considerations are important in and to our capacity to address the suffering believer pastorally. And yet we must end on a note of caution.

Suffering presents a real challenge to the pastor-preacher who would address it. The pain of suffering, or for that matter anguish of any kind, can close people or organizations down so that they are not open to a word of comfort. Years ago Rollo May said that anxiety is disjunctive, that is, that by its very nature it tends to disconnect people and to make them unavailable to one another. The same thing is true of suffering. Suffering, with its intense pain and its own preoccupations, can isolate the sufferer and cause him or her to withdraw both emotionally and cognitively. This reaction is often accentuated by the anesthetic effect of shock, which shuts the person down to provide protection from a shattered world. Dealing with or reaching the suffering believer, therefore, is often not easy and sometimes is not possible.

At the same time and in apparent contradiction, we must also say that somewhere along the line suffering may make the sufferer available for help. Years ago Howard Stone identified the "heightened psychological accessibility of an individual in crisis."[11] Persons who suffer may be emotionally ready to reflect on their situation and to grow in ways that the stable individual is not. Similarly, when a congregation or community is knocked off balance by suffering, when there is a need to restore equilibrium, the defenses of those involved may be down. If the individual or the congregation trusts the pastor-preacher, they may be ready to listen to the Word of God and be comforted by its promises.

3

The Church's Attempt to Address Suffering

CHRISTIANS, OF COURSE, HAVE SUFFERED down through the ages. And through the ages the church has tried to address those who suffer. It has had the audacity—or the faith—to believe that it has an answer to suffering, not one that will make suffering go away but one that can empower the person to go through suffering.

One of the church's chief means of addressing suffering has been the Sunday morning sermon. In the twentieth century, a variety of attempts have been made to link preaching and pastoral care so that the sermon would become a more effective vehicle of congregational care. Many pastors have sought to fine-tune their preaching to address God's healing word to suffering believers. Known variously as life-situation preaching, therapeutic preaching, and preaching to personal issues, this type of pulpit address has flourished, has withered, and has been reinvigorated repeatedly in the past eighty years.

In this chapter we want to take a historical look at the church's attempt to address the person in suffering. In other words, we want to focus on what we are calling pastoral preaching. We will mine the gems that are found in significant attempts to preach pastorally, but we will also begin to craft a better way to address human needs, one that remains reverent to the Word of God while also being attentive to those who suffer. There are some key players in the history of pastoral preaching.

The Antecedents of Pastoral Preaching

Harry Emerson Fosdick

In 1928 two people, one a German theologian named Karl Barth and the other an American preacher named Harry Emerson Fosdick, wrote on the subject of preaching. Both of them put their stamp on preaching for the next fifty years, so much so that their influence continues into the present century. For decades the neo-orthodoxy of Barth and the liberalism of Fosdick seemed to posit competition between the two men, but in fact the critique of each other's position helped the pastor in the parish to speak God's Word to the worshiping community. With Barth the pastor was called back to the Word of God; with Fosdick the preacher was challenged to attend to the life situation of the parishioner. This tension, of course, did not prevent some pastor-preachers from falling on one side or the other.

Horace Bushnell (1802–1876) and Phillips Brooks (1835–1893) are remembered as outstanding preachers who were attuned to the roles of pastor and preacher, but Fosdick (1873–1969) deserves credit for exciting a whole generation of preachers with the challenge of addressing the pastoral needs of a congregation. Riverside Church on Morningside Heights in New York City, which was erected in 1931 as a tribute to Fosdick's ministry, stands as a physical reminder of his influence.

Fosdick himself went through some intense internal turmoil. He had an emotional breakdown in his first year at Union Theological Seminary, and later he tried to commit suicide; consequently, his development as a preacher took a different trajectory than most of his contemporaries. In his short essay in *Harper's Magazine* entitled "What Is the Matter with Preaching?" he criticized the expository preaching of his day.[1] He charged that it spent most of the time on a historical study of a scriptural verse, "ending with some appended practical application."[2] Sometimes, he observed, the preacher never escaped the confines of the text, so that the outcome was Bible study and not preaching. Fosdick was convinced that Bible-bound preaching was intrinsically irrelevant. "Only the preacher," he wrote, "proceeds still upon the idea that folk come to church desperately anxious to discover what happened to the Jebusites."[3]

Fosdick was equally dismayed by what he labeled "topical preaching," namely, discourses on public issues "such as divorce, Bolshevism, America's foreign policy, the new aviation, or the latest book."[4] To Fosdick, such preaching was not worthy of the name.

Instead of beginning with either a biblical text or a current issue, Fosdick maintained that preachers should begin with the personal problems of people.

> Every sermon should have for its main business the head-on constructive meeting of some problem which was puzzling minds, burdening consciences, distracting lives, and no sermon which so met a real human difficulty, with light to throw on it and help to win a victory over it, could possibly be futile.[5]

For Fosdick the test of whether the sermon was good or not was determined by how many listeners wished to see him for personal counseling. Counseling fed Fosdick's preaching, giving him insight into the hopes and fears of worshipers, but it also became a criterion of its effectiveness. Preaching and counseling should merge in the sermon. Even though an entire congregation is addressed in a single sermon, the preacher should speak to the congregation as individuals. In Fosdick's view the preacher is primarily a personal counselor.[6]

Fosdick's "project method," in which the preacher begins with the listener's difficulties, led to several problems. If many didactic sermons never got out of the Bible, many sermons in the Fosdick tradition never got into the Bible or, if they did, they simply contained verses that could be applied to the problem. This "proof text" approach often meant that the verses were used out of context to support what the preacher really wanted to say.

Fosdick's virtual conflation of counseling and preaching also had its deleterious effect on the counseling side of the equation. Pastoral care is integral to the shepherding of a congregation, and pastoral care may include some brief counseling, but extensive psychological counseling is best left to trained counselors. Furthermore, Fosdick's test of the effectiveness of a given sermon—how many listeners want to see the preacher for personal counseling afterward—has caused generations of clergy to feel like failures.

Fosdick was correct in believing that preaching is essential to a pastor's shepherding of a congregation. He was also correct in believing that preachers whose sermons routinely bog down in the exegesis of the text tend to be irrelevant both to the felt needs of listeners and to their deeper real needs. To be emulated, however, was Fosdick's practice of picturing particular troubled persons as he prepared to preach. His silent prayer before each sermon was, "O God, some one person here needs what I am going to say. Help me to reach him."[7] Fosdick was sometimes extravagant in his expectation of what the sermon might do. He strove for a "transformation of personality." He wrote, "The real sermon must do more than discuss joy—it must produce it. All powerful preaching is creative. It actually brings to pass in the lives of the congregation that thing that it talks about."[8] In an age that tends to undervalue the power of the Word, Fosdick's sense of the potential power of preaching is a healthy corrective.

The Positive Preachers

The "positive preachers" of the twentieth century seem to descend from Fosdick, at least in part. The blend of liberal theology and therapeutic preaching continued in Norman Vincent Peale's cathedral, the Marble Collegiate Church in New York City, in Robert Schuller's Crystal Cathedral in Orange County, California, and in many other pulpits in America. The triumph of the therapeutic, often at the expense of the Bible and the gospel, was realized in the psychologically oriented society of the latter decades of the last century.

However, positive preaching has a lineage earlier than Fosdick.[9] The Reverend Warren Evans of Boston, an ex-Methodist who became enchanted with the teachings of Emanuel Swedenborg, published a book in 1869 called *The Mental Cure*. Evans argued that healing comes as the fruit of what Swedenborg called "divine influx" and love. Evans's book influenced Mary Baker Eddy, who in 1875 published *Science and Health with Key to the Scriptures*. Eddy argued that disease does not exist and that God, as Supreme Mind, could not be resisted. Her followers gathered together and chartered the Church of Christ (Scientist) in 1879.[10]

While Christian Science was the most conspicuous form of mental cure in the twentieth century, the Unity School of Christianity, founded in Kansas City by Charles Filmore and his wife, Myrtle, was more pervasive. Unity reached a million homes each month through eight magazines and numerous pamphlets. It broadened the concern of positive thinking from health and healing to promise unlimited.

The Depression in the late 1920s spawned Dale Carnegie's self-improvement program and his famous book, *How to Win Friends and Influence People.* It also spawned a religious manifestation of the gospel of success.

A young New Jersey pastor felt unequipped to do counseling, because the psychology he had been taught in seminary seemed overly academic and too theoretical for practical use in a congregational ministry. When Norman Vincent Peale came to Marble Collegiate Church, the Reformed Church in America congregation on Fifth Avenue in New York, he consulted with Dr. Smiley Blanton, who had been trained in Vienna by Sigmund Freud. By 1937 Peale had organized his Religio-Psychiatric Clinic, with a staff of ministers, psychoanalysts, psychologists, doctors, and social workers.

Peale himself was not attracted to personal counseling as much as he was to mass communication. He preached regularly at Marble Collegiate while traveling perpetually to speak. His second book, *You Can Win,* was indicative of future directions. By 1946 the circulation of his printed sermons reached 17,000 per week. *Guideposts* magazine was started, reaching a circulation of eight hundred thousand in the late 1950s. *The Power of Positive Thinking,* first published in 1952, became the bible of the movement and rose to the top of the best-seller list and stayed there for two years.

While Fosdick's theology was liberal, many theologians deemed Peale's heretical. In an article in the *Saturday Review of Literature* entitled "Pitchman in the Pulpit," one writer described "Pealism" as "a puerile, vitiated, shallow revival of Pelagianism."[11] Peale's thought was a sophisticated form of mental cure in which the unacceptable messages of sin, suffering, and injustice in the world were studiously avoided. Sin, it was asserted, evoked guilt in listeners, and guilt, resulting in low self-esteem, was deemed responsible for most human ills. Peale's basic message was "think differently and life will be different." Problems were buffered with happiness and humor, and Peale's sermons overflowed with *Guidepost*-like success stories, in which people overcame all sorts of obstacles on the way to getting their lives together.

Like Peale, the Reverend Robert H. Schuller is a prominent representative of what is termed "healthy-minded religion." He advocates what he calls "possibility thinking," which is rooted in a theology of self-esteem. In his rapidly growing area of Garden Grove, California, he found many unchurched people who were not at all prepared to listen to God-talk.[12] In preaching to them, and later in his televised ministry, he avoided any references to sin and guilt. Instead, Schuller emphasized a positive view of human nature and sought to build up self-worth, pride, and self-esteem.

Schuller's gospel of possibility thinking is inevitably personal, dealing with problems that seem ideally suited to simple solutions. Of course, human issues like jealousy, fear, and worry should be addressed from time to time in preaching, but when they are not seen as symptoms of a deeper malady, as manifestations of our failure to trust in God, they become manageable challenges that can be overcome on the way to a pain-free life. The sermon itself is reduced to a piece of pop psychology, abounding with simplistic solutions: "Turn your scars into stars. It will make you a better or a bitter person; it all depends on you. Reverse them; turn your hurt into a halo."[13]

If sin and guilt are neglected in Schuller's preaching, so also are the death and resurrection of Jesus. Being "soft on sin," Schuller is also "light on grace." In search of "possibility messages" in Scripture, Schuller and other positive preachers give the heart of the gospel a once-over-lightly treatment. The message that God's Son needed to die for fallen humanity and to be raised again to overcome death becomes hopelessly dated and offensive. Positive preachers reduce the gospel to a program of self-help, which God is said to approve or even desire. Like Peale, Schuller's theology and preaching have been subject to severe criticism.

> [The criticisms] include lack of depth and variety in his almost one-track message of possibility-thinking, his near total inattention to sin, especially its institutional and systemic dimension; his refusal to address in sermons serious public moral concerns that are an offense to the gospel; his inordinate emphasis on success, especially wealth, which often seems for him to be more a contributor to self-esteem than its by-product; and his tendency at times to identify the Christian way with the American way.[14]

Schuller's message is not totally Pollyanna. In moderation a sense of self-worth and self-esteem is healthy. And at its best, possibility-thinking is a resolve to approach problems constructively, to make the most of what life sends, and to overcome adversity. In the end the message is still a plan of self-help. In the short run it may encourage people with ego strength and a firm sense of self-esteem. When their optimism wanes in the face of reality, the weekly "fix" of sermon and song may keep them going. But for believers who bear a heavy or chronic burden or who suffer from low self-esteem, a temporary sense of euphoria brought on by a slap on the back will not get them through the valley. Douglas John Hall says it best:

> However "successful" all these theories and messages may seem to the affluent and basically healthy persons to whose quest for "peace of mind" they are obviously directed, they are reduced to dust and ashes by the cry of one child dying of cancer, one woman tortured until she betrays her friends.[15]

In the end self-help is a hindrance to the gospel, because it centers on human resources rather than on the Word of God. Schuller's injunction to "turn your scars into stars. . . . It all depends on you" sums up the philosophy.[16] "His theology is as simple as equating sin with negative thoughts and original sin with self-doubt."[17] But the Bible does not see sin as negative thoughts or self-doubt. It sees sin as a rebellion that moved God to expose the Son to the depths of human suffering, even death on a cross. The suffering of the Son is the really good news, for by his "scars," not by our "stars," we are healed.

The Development of Pastoral Preaching

While the date of Fosdick's seminal article was 1928, it was not until the decade of the 1940s that teachers of preaching recognized pastoral preaching as a separate type of sermon. A survey of sixty-eight homiletics textbooks written by American-born teachers of homiletics between 1834 and 1954 indicates that the life-situation sermon per se was not referred to in texts written prior to 1944.[18] Halford Luccock, in his influential book *In the Minister's Workshop*, argues that the life-situation or pastoral sermon originates in the experience of the listening congregation rather than in either a current issue or a biblical text. For Luccock, this insight helped to distinguish pastoral preaching from both expository preaching and social-issue preaching. Luccock's work helped pastors utilize this new type of pulpit communication.

The pastoral psychology and Clinical Pastoral Education movements of the 1940s and 1950s sparked an interest in, and an examination of, the relationship between pastoral care and preaching. The conviction grew that caring is not limited to hospital visitation and one-to-one pastoral conversations but is manifested in the entire range of pastoral duty, including preaching. "Every time the preached message confronts and forms personal need in the light of the gospel, pastoral care occurs."[19]

As the pastoral preaching movement matured, it sought to embrace the insights of psychology while avoiding the extremes of over- and under-valuing a pastoral approach. Its more thoughtful practitioners have renounced extravagant claims for such preaching. Pastoral preaching is not "counseling on a group scale," as Fosdick said, nor is it to be reduced to problem solving from the pulpit, as positive thinkers have implied. At its best, pastoral preaching is biblically grounded, theologically sound, and pastorally sensitive.

In its development, pastoral preaching has manifested certain flaws. These flaws have been identified by thoughtful practitioners and teachers of preaching and need to be underscored here.

1. Life-situation sermons are often more topical than textual, with the Bible used more as a resource than as a source. In a biblically illiterate age, most sermons should emerge from and demonstrate a profound engagement with Scripture.

2. All human problems do not have solutions or answers, certainly no complete ones. To suggest that they do is neither true to Scripture nor helpful to troubled believers.

3. Some pastoral sermons substitute pop psychology for the gospel. Even when this is avoided, many leap unsuccessfully from a personal/psychological problem to a theological response without making a legitimate connection between the two.

4. While clergy indeed take cues from their own needs and struggles, preachers must avoid allowing their problems and their story to take over the sermon, turning the pulpit into a confessional booth.

5. Moralism in the form of principles to follow, success programs, general advice, or even biblical "truths" applied as formulas are contrary to a sound understanding of how God works in the lives of persons. There are no "magic potions" for human problems, and sermons should not suggest otherwise.

6. Pastoral preachers often focus on one-to-one issues to the neglect of public affairs. Indeed, this narrow personalism leads to a deafening silence about the implications of the gospel for public life.

7. While clothing Jesus in contemporary terms to make him more available to congregations, many pastoral preachers ignore biblical claims for Jesus' divinity, resulting in a weak or nonexistent Christology.

Contemporary Contributions to Pastoral Preaching

There are two contemporary attempts to relate preaching and pastoral care in service to pastoral preaching. The first writer is primarily a pastoral theorist, the second one primarily a homiletician.

Donald Capps, in *Pastoral Counseling and Preaching: A Quest for an Integrated Ministry,* does not set out to contribute to what we are calling pastoral preaching.[20] Instead, he is concerned about the tendency to see preaching and pastoral counseling as two separate and distinct activities of ministry. He believes that the two activities are not antithetical to each other but that, in fact, they are "two foci of an integrated ministry,"[21] and therefore they can mutually enrich each other. He bases his position on the fact that both activities, unlike other functions of ministry, have a formal structure. They occur at a definable time and carry with them definable expectations.

Capps presses his analysis and concludes that the formal structure of both activities has four common features. Each activity identifies the problem to be addressed, locates the problem in its larger context, diagnoses or assesses the problem theologically, and considers or offers a strategy to deal with the problem. Capps is careful to describe the particular way in which both preaching and pastoral counseling go through these four steps, but he ends with the notion that their similarity is greater than their difference, which means that they are related to and can contribute to one another.

Capps's analysis is of interest to us not just because he clarifies the structural similarities that exist between preaching and pastoral counseling but more so because he makes an important contribution to our discussion of pastoral preaching. His four steps, if followed faithfully, may yield a pastoral sermon, one that uses the resources of both preaching and pastoral care to communicate or mediate God's care to the needy person. A close look at his four steps clarifies the point.

First, there is the identification of the problem, not just the apparent problem but the one that seems to be the very source of the trouble. The problem might be of a personal nature, which the pastor has come to know from a counseling situation, or it might be of a more general nature, one that derives from the pastor's observation of the congregation as a whole. Capps illustrates this first step by citing one of Martin Luther King's sermons. King points out that while Christians are not to be conformed to this world, often that is precisely what they do. Instead of being transformed by the renewing of their minds, Christians are conditioned by the world to follow the thinking of the majority. The identification of this as the problem sets King up to deal more precisely with society's pressure to conform.

Second, according to Capps, the pastor needs to reconstruct the problem, that is, to explore its various facets and to put it in its wider context. This step adds concrete detail to the situation and clarifies why the problem is troubling and deserves to be taken seriously. In this step, Martin Luther King, according to Capps, "enumerates some of the specific pressures that the contemporary world exerts on people to conform."[22] He observes that the problem is often especially prevalent in the church and that the church's conformity often serves to support and even to reinforce the status quo.

The third step involves what Capps calls diagnostic interpretation. It is an assessment of the problem or, more fully, it is bringing together the various partial interpretations that may have been ventured in the second step and forming them into a coherent and incisive whole. Capps notes that it is at this point more than at previous points that biblical or theological resources may be used to interpret the problem. King illustrates the point when he maintains that nonconformity by itself is not necessarily good or bad. It is good and serves a creative purpose only when it follows "Paul's formula for constructive nonconformity," that is, only when it proceeds from a transformed life and represents a "new mental outlook."[23]

The final step in the sermon is what is called pastoral intervention. It represents a proposed plan of action. It lays out a strategy that is often worked out in reciprocal relation with the previous step, for diagnosis and intervention are intimately tied together. Where no final solution can be offered, the pastor is to offer a clear strategy and to suggest helpful ways in which the congregation can respond to (live with) the problem. King's fourth step is an invitation to join "a dedicated circle of transformed nonconformists." He points out that membership in this circle may be costly and involve pain, but he challenges the audience to follow the "more excellent way."[24]

Capps achieves what he sets out to do, namely, to show that there are structural similarities between preaching and pastoral counseling that can contribute to the mutual enrichment of both activities. The two activities may approach the four steps in different ways and in fact may illuminate a particular situation from different angles, but their common structure means that they can work together and even supplement each other in the quest for an integrated ministry.

Capps does not go on to use the affinity between preaching and pastoral counseling to create an approach to pastoral preaching. The four steps may yield a pastoral sermon, but it is up to the minister to make it work. It helps if the minister has a clear understanding of the conceptual or theoretical issues, but more important, it is imperative to have a pastor who is attentive to God's Word and a preacher who is attentive to the needs of the people.

In the end, Capps does not give us a formula for pastoral preaching. He has not even examined the possibility in any detail. We turn, therefore, to a second writer, to one who is primarily a homiletician.

Unlike Capps, J. Randall Nichols does not dwell on the relationship between preaching and pastoral counseling. He notes some of the differences that exist between the two, but he finds a point of interaction between them in the concept of restoration. He believes that the central task of ministry is to restore, to bring back something that has been lost. He also believes that in pursuing this task some of the "painful dichotomies" between preaching and pastoral care "can become creative tensions instead of crippling dilemmas."[25] His entire book *The Restoring Word: Preaching as Pastoral Communication* is an explication of this belief, with special sensitivity to the hearer who sits in the pew. This sensitivity leads him to center on pastoral preaching, which he defines as "the homiletical occasion when . . . a sermon addresses or impacts the personally invested concerns of its hearers."[26]

According to Nichols, preaching can be pastoral in three ways: The hearer can perceive the sermon that way, the pastor can set out to address personal concerns, or the subject matter of the sermon may deal with an issue—for example, divorce—that has "pastoral import." In "candid moments," Nichols admits, he thinks that "pastoral preaching is as much as anything a posture, a sensitivity, an attitude,"[27] for this inner stance focuses the mind on a personal concern of the hearer and shapes the way in which the pastor crafts the sermon. In our terms, Nichols is saying that not only is it up to the minister to make a sermon pastoral, but also it is imperative that the minister be pastoral.

Nichols goes on to examine preaching, specifically pastoral preaching, in great detail. We need to follow his discussion, because at each turn he sheds light on pastoral preaching. He starts by considering nine ways in which preaching can be either helpful or harmful. His discussion includes items like helping people to discover God's grace instead of telling them about it, helping them to move from unproductive guilt to realistic responsibility, helping them to see that their lives make sense and are meaningful, and helping them to get beyond low self-esteem and see themselves as "a new and loved person in Jesus Christ." All nine items have a common concern. They are Nichols's assessment of what it means to be pastorally, or really psychologically, sensitive to people and help them move toward genuine restoration. In other words, the discussion is a good example of using therapeutic insights and homiletical truths to construct a baseline for pastoral preaching. For this reason, we will return to some of Nichols's nine points when we take up specific instances of suffering in the chapters that follow.

Nichols continues his examination of pastoral preaching by turning to the preacher. Is the preacher priest or prophet, or in other words, is he or she pastor or proclaimer? Nichols does not minimize the difference between the two roles; in fact, he pinpoints their difference very precisely, but he does not think that we have to choose between the two. He sees a dialectical tension between them and believes there is a type of communication that transcends the mundane to become life-determining. In this moment, priest and prophet, the concern for human brokenness and the concern for God's activity, are in creative tension. This is also the moment called pastoral preaching.

And what does pastoral preaching do? Nichols answers this question by drawing a parallel between the functions of preaching and of psychotherapy. He does not subscribe to Fosdick's belief that "preaching is a 'form of therapy,' "[28] but he does maintain that the therapeutic situation can help us understand the restoring role of proclamation in preaching. Like the therapist, the pastoral preacher creates a sanctuary in which the parishioner has permission to examine his or her world, to see it in another light, and to do whatever it takes to get a better and more hopeful grip on the situation. Both the therapist and the pastoral preacher are trying to restore the person to a greater degree of wholeness and a more fulfilling life. Nichols puts some of his thoughts into theological language, but he is not especially eager to do so. In fact, he thinks "it is short-sighted to limit what we mean by 'proclamation of the gospel' to theological *content.*" He is more concerned to help the troubled person "live out [the] 'gospel.' "[29]

Nichols continues his perspectival survey of preaching by focusing on the use of the self in preaching. This consideration has special relevance to pastoral preaching, for surely the self of the preacher must be involved in any attempt to address personal issues. Nichols sees two undesirable extremes: On the one hand, there is the attempt to remove any evidence of the self from the style or strategy of the sermon; on the other hand, there is the temptation to make the self the center of the sermon. Over against these extremes, Nichols believes there is an "appropriate, even necessary, use of the self " in the whole process: in the choosing of the text, in the pastoral strategy for the sermon, and in the preparation and delivery of the end product. Nichols cannot prescribe the exact use of the self in the pulpit, but he surely adds the preacher's human touch to the attempt to address "the personally invested concerns of " the hearers.

Finally, there is the context in which pastoral preaching takes place, namely, worship. Worship takes place in and through an order of service, and Nichols deals with the constituent parts of the service, but what he really seems to be talking about is worshiping, the posture of being in "the presence of the intimately personal while at the same time [being in the presence of] the mysteriously holy."[30] He examines worship in this sense and tries to lift out the ways in which it, along with preaching, contributes to the pastoral task of ministry. His labored thought can be boiled down to three basic points: Worship is a call out of our daily life (regular social structures) to see ourselves in relation to the sacred, so that we might be transformed and then "carry the fruits of that transformation back" to our weekday worlds. Second, worship is a series of interlocking "parts" that lead us through the experience and help to make it a "unique restorative experience." Third, each of the various parts of the service, like confession, creed, prayer, and so on, has its own message or personal address. For example, confession invites the person to own his or her own culpability and to move toward restoration by taking responsibility for what he or she has done or not done instead of denying it. In any case, Nichols maintains that together the various parts form "a liturgy of restoration,"[31] which, of course, is a fitting context for the purposes of pastoral preaching.

Nichols gives us a more direct look at some of the constituent parts of pastoral preaching. He is especially helpful in terms of the mechanics of communication and is less helpful in terms of its content. In other words, if pastoral preaching means, as it does for us, an interweaving of concrete situation and God's Word, Nichols focuses on the former to the neglect of the latter.

Conclusion

Our task has been to see how the church has sought to address the problematic side of the human situation, specifically in terms of pastoral preaching. We have clarified the historical context in which pastoral preaching emerges as a distinct type of address even as we have tried to locate it in the overall pastoral strategy of ministry. We are now ready to zero in on the pastor's attempt to be pastoral to the suffering believer.

4

The Pastoral Response to Suffering

IN CHAPTER 1 WE REFERRED BRIEFLY TO THE TEACHER who lost her husband to a bicycle accident in a southwestern state. Mrs. Demise, as we will call her, was traumatized by her husband's death. She realized that she could have prevented her husband from going on the trip if she had "put up enough fuss." Her agony was increased when her husband's family called on her after the funeral and demanded that she return several items that had been given to the husband by the family.

Mrs. Demise could not turn to her two adopted sons for help. The one had disowned the family several years earlier and had not been heard from since. The other was immersed in his own grief and had no energy to deal with her sorrow. So when the pastor appeared at her home, he was met with a barrage of pent-up grief: "It's grim. That's the only way I can describe it. Grim." With these words, Mrs. Demise began to pour out her grief and reach out for help. She looked to the minister for comfort and help, trying to find an answer to a seemingly senseless situation.

Fortunately, the minister was sensitive to her need. In fact, that is why he came to the home in the first place—to offer Mrs. Demise an attentive ear and a tender heart. He invited her to retell her story, how she first heard of her husband's death, how she reacted to the shocking news, how she had to make tough decisions about bringing the body back and finding a place of burial. In all of this, it became apparent that Mrs. Demise was alone in her grief, bereft of family who could stand by her and isolated from most of her neighbors and friends. The minister heard in Mrs. Demise's grief the cry of the writer of Ecclesiastes, "Vanity of vanities. All is vanity."

The minister listened to her story without trying to minimize her grief or short-circuit her sorrow. He stood by her, hearing what she said without judging it and being with her as she railed against the unfairness of fate. He had been trained in the art of pastoral care, and through this ministry he was attempting to walk with Mrs. Demise in her hour of sorrow. Without reassuring her by using easy-to-say words, he was hoping to witness to God's care by being a concrete incarnation of it.

The pastor's one-to-one care of Mrs. Demise is a vital part of his ministry to her—so vital that other more public forms of ministry cannot replace it. At the same time, other forms of ministry, for example, preaching, are needed to minister fully to Mrs. Demise's situation. Not everything that Mrs. Demise needs can be supplied in a pastoral visit, however helpful that visit may be. When Mrs. Demise comes to church, she is "looking for something more," even though she may not be consciously aware of what it is. In fact, being in church may raise questions or bring up hurts that were not potentiated in the pastor's one-to-one ministry. Now that she is sitting in the pew, she waits for the pastor to address her needs as he or she preaches God's Word.

When the pastor enters the pulpit, hopefully he or she will not put pastoral care in a separate compartment and find no relation between caring and preaching. We also hope that the pastor will not conflate the two forms of ministry into one and with Fosdick assume that preaching is nothing more than counseling. We believe that the task is to give credence to both forms of ministry by recognizing their similarities and differences even while trying to combine them into a single act of ministry called pastoral preaching.

We are getting ahead of ourselves. We are focusing on the relationship between preaching and pastoral care as it relates to pastoral preaching. That relationship is a primary concern, but before we get there, we need to put pastoral preaching into a wider context. In chapter 2 we discussed the various resources that are available to our pastoral ministry, resources like baptism, the psalms, and prayer. All of these resources have to do with what we will call the pastoral relationship, that is, with the pastor's ongoing interaction with members of his or her flock.

The Pastoral Relationship

The pastoral relationship takes many different forms under many different circumstances. For some, the relationship of pastor and parishioner will be formal with little if any private conversation. For others, the struggle with illness, hospitalization, or family stress may precipitate more intimate contact and conversation. A counseling relationship may even develop beyond the pastor's normal ministry of prayer and consolation.

The breadth of the pastoral relationship can be observed from other angles. In the educational ministry of the congregation, the pastor has an opportunity to help believers engage profound problems with societal and faith dimensions. The church should be a safe place to tackle difficult issues like racial prejudice, sexuality, and various kinds of social injustices. In the organizational life of the congregation, situations come up that evoke a consideration of suffering. For example, declining membership, financial shortfalls, lack of vision, loss of a sense of mission, and conflict within the congregation may precipitate deep distress. In many activities of the church, the pastor is immersed in relationships in which he or she is placed in the midst of some measure of suffering. He or she is in a pastoral relationship, whether or not it is called by that name.

In this relationship the pastor has an opportunity, we might even say a duty, to probe feelings, images, and interpretations that signal distress. Reason and emotion are governed by different kinds of "logic," but they are linked in the lives of people. The mind needs to cope with suffering on a feeling level just as feelings require perception-cognition to make sense of our suffering. Questions that seem innocent or rational often tend to be laced with anger, guilt, or despair. "Why does Jane get by with angry outbursts when I don't?" Answers are demanded, sometimes quick answers, to explain the apparent injustice and to restore some sense of balance.

Initially, the role of the pastor or helping person is not to give answers but to listen. The demand for answers is best deflected, lest theoretical formulations grasped in panic prove partial or simplistic in retrospect. By patient listening, by containing one's own feelings, by communicating calm and control, the pastor helps to keep the level of distress within tolerable limits.

The pastoral relationship is often crucial to pastoral preaching. It is that relationship in which the pastor can observe firsthand the exact nature of the person's suffering. What is the sufferer asking? How is the family, the congregation, or the broader community baffled by the situation that oppresses them? What strengths and weaknesses do they bring to the crisis? The emotional intensity of their questions or queries often indicates the urgency of their need.

The pastoral relationship can also reveal the theology of suffering that is implicit in the parishioner's struggle.

> Frequently, this intuitive theology is a far cry from the coherent cross-centered faith of the church. It may be inchoate, comprised of random bits of Sunday-school memories, unrelated images, cultural aphorisms, and person philosophy. This theology may be discernible in crisis if at no other time.[1]

Our pastoral preaching should take full account of the theological perspective of persons who suffer. Helping people make sense of life, including facing its baffling and conflicted parts squarely, is one of the chief purposes of pastoral preaching. We cannot help them reframe their understanding of the situation unless we know the belief system on which they rest their case. A pastoral relationship can address both the emotions and the theological perspective that sufferers hold. Pastoral preaching, when based on concrete instances of pastoral care, can address sufferers where they are.

Clarification of the pastoral relationship allows us to return to the two ministerial activities that weigh heavy in pastoral preaching. We need to describe some of the major differences that exist between preaching and pastoral care.

Practical Differences

Pastoral care and preaching do not combine easily into a pastoral sermon.[2] The differences between them are significant, and they need to be respected. Among other things, the differences seem to derive from the fact that pastoral care is a private ministry and preaching is a public ministry. This disparity confronts the pastor who seeks to preach pastorally with at least five practical issues.

First, each ministry addresses a different audience. As a public ministry, preaching focuses on and seeks to address a whole fellowship of people, while a private ministry like pastoral counseling is concerned about an individual or a small group within the church. The difference is more than numerical. It means that preaching addresses a more complex and less monolithic reality, making communication more precarious while offering fewer opportunities to clarify misunderstandings.

More important, the interests and needs of an individual in community are often different than the interests of the same individual in a one-to-one relationship. The shift is often intangible and hard to perceive, but it is as real as the distinction between the public self and the private self. An individual will expose certain things in private that he or she would be loathe to expose in public. In addition, the individual attends to different aspects of himself or herself as he or she moves in the private sphere compared to the public sphere. This means that the object of our pastoral concern may change as the setting changes. The needs of a mourner in a public service are often not the same as his or her needs in a private visit. Pastoral preaching must be attentive to this change; otherwise, a pastor may try to address private needs in a public ceremony and find himself or herself less than appropriate or comforting.

A second difference between pastoral care and preaching has to do with communication. While preaching usually takes the form of proclamation as announcement, pastoral care and counseling usually take the form of proclamation as incarnate Word. Or as Lloyd M. Perry and Charles M. Sell put it: "Pastoral counseling and preaching communicate the same reality, but preaching does it through the spoken word while counseling does it through the relationship of counselee and counselor."[3]

Neither form of proclamation is of automatic or absolute value. Which form is more appropriate and potentially more effective is determined in part by the needs and circumstances of the parishioner. In terms of pastoral preaching, this means that what is usually conveyed through a relationship of embodied care must be made effective through verbal announcement. It also means that pastoral preaching is not necessarily sufficient by itself. It must be seen as part of a larger ministry in which pastoral care may need both to precede and to follow it.

Preaching declares what is believed; counseling deals with what is experienced. This third difference is not categorical, but it says something about how the listener relates to the gospel. In preaching the pastor witnesses to or proclaims the message of God, whether or not the listener is in an existential position to affirm or accept it. Preaching is the community of faith declaring its faith and thereby inviting the troubled parishioner to live by the promise, even though his or her immersion in grief, doubt, or some other struggle may limit his or her ability to believe it.

In distinction, counseling as private ministry is concerned about the existential situation of the person. It explores what is operative in the present moment and witnesses to the message of God only as that message is relevant to the present world of the parishioner. Pastoral preaching is called upon to bridge the gap between these two orientations, to speak the Word but to speak it in a way and at a time when it impacts on the existential world of the parishioner.

A fourth difference is that a public ministry focuses on what is visible to all or what can be known by all, while a private ministry focuses on what is hidden or what should be known only by a select few.

The distinction raises the question of confidentiality and indicates that in pastoral preaching the pastor must respect and preserve the parishioner's right to privacy. What is private cannot be made public in any identifiable way. Assuming this, the pastor must still deal with the question, "How can I articulate and preach to situations that must remain private?" An obvious solution is to disguise the situation by altering all identifiable facts. Sometimes this can be accomplished by conflating several situations into a single case, though this procedure does not necessarily prevent sensitive parishioners from feeling exposed.

A better way to protect anonymity is to generalize the pastoral situation and to deal with universal human needs to which, hopefully, individuals can relate. The best way, though, may be to address the effects of a situation without dealing with the situation itself. For example, a pastor could deal with the aftermath of a suicide in the congregation without elaborating the details of the suicide. In this way, the pastor can speak a pastoral word to parishioners without betraying their right to privacy.

The use of concrete situations in pastoral preaching raises another question—namely, how detailed the pastor should become when describing a specific situation. If the details of the case are too intricate or too shocking, the pastor may overwhelm, or at least turn off, the congregation. In pastoral counseling this issue becomes a conscious/unconscious consideration. If the counselor gets too far ahead of the client and enters forbidden territory, he or she may turn off the client and raise the client's defenses. The same issue inheres in pastoral preaching. The pastor must know where boundaries are and when he or she stands in danger of overstepping them. If a wrong step is taken, the congregation may react to both the invasion and the indiscretion.

Finally, in pastoral preaching we need to be concerned about how much of the personal situation can be answered in and through preaching. If a serious problem is raised, some kind of helpful and believable answer is necessary; otherwise, the pastor may increase the parishioner's sense of hopelessness and reflect negatively on the power of the gospel. Given this danger, preachers like Robert Schuller are at least headed in the right direction when they imply that the best that the pastor can do when preaching to personal issues is to instill a sense of hope by changing the way the troubled person sees his or her situation. Schuller, and other positive preachers, strive to change negative thinking into positive thinking, to help the individual "turn scars into stars." On one level this endeavor can be naive and simplistic, when pop psychology and enthusiasm are substituted for the firm hope of the gospel, but on another level it can be a life-saving help to those who have lost vision and hope.

Pastoral care has employed a similar technique during much of its history. It has encouraged the parishioner to turn from the dark side of a situation long enough to see that God is working in and through it. Martin Luther is a notable example. In his *Letters of Spiritual Counsel,* he often tried to get the troubled person to focus on God's presence or promise. To Matthias Weller, who suffered from melancholy, he wrote, "Listen, then, to what we are saying to you in God's name: Rejoice in Christ, who is your gracious Lord and Redeemer. Let him bear your burdens, for he assuredly cares for you."[4] Recently, Donald Capps has extended our knowledge of this approach to pastoral care by devoting an entire book to it.[5] I think it is important to acknowledge that the approach is employed not only in pastoral care but also in the pulpit. In both cases, it can be a realistic assessment of our human situation and a humble acknowledgment of our inability to change it. That alone may help the troubled parishioner to live with his or her condition.

We have not exhausted the practical differences between pastoral care and preaching, but we have laid out some issues that inhere in any attempt to combine them into pastoral preaching. We have found that whatever else pastoral preaching does or is, it must relate faith and life, that is, it must relate what the church proclaims with what the troubled parishioner is experiencing, and it must do it in a way that is both faithful to God's Word and attentive to the parishioner's concrete situation. The point can be put another way: In pastoral preaching the minister must be both pastor and preacher. Some ministers believe that the difference between these two roles is very real, and they have trouble combining the two into a single occasion. Other ministers, while acknowledging the difference, believe that there are similarities between the two roles, and they find it easier and more natural to form the two into a single entity.

Toward a Better Way

In chapter 3 we laid out a seven-count indictment against early forms of pastoral preaching. The indictment prompts us to try to find a better way to conceive of pastoral preaching. A better way begins with a clear understanding of the nature of preaching itself. We believe that preaching is primarily speaking to a worshiping congregation about God and God's gracious activity in the lives of human beings. This simple definition serves both to shape the sermon and to help the preacher avoid most of the pitfalls mentioned above.

The design of the sermon is initiated by posing a question of the biblical text: What is God doing here? The answer, framed as a crisp declarative sentence, keeps the sermon focused on God's activity. Thus God, Christ, or the Holy Spirit becomes the subject of the sermon sentence and of the resulting sermon. The action inheres in the verb: What is God saying or doing, first in the text and then in the present? The sermon sentence should underscore what God is doing here and now in a present-day situation of human need. These elements can be illustrated by referring to a sermon one of us preached to a Philadelphia congregation from John 21:1-19, the *Revised Common Lectionary* text appointed for the Third Sunday of Easter 2001.

Text Sentence: In a situation of human failure, the risen Christ revealed himself to discouraged disciples in word and action, challenging Peter to feed the sheep.

Sermon Sentence: In a situation of human failure today, the risen Christ reveals himself to discouraged disciples in word and action, challenging them to active discipleship in witness and service.

These elements indicate that whether a given sermon is born in the gestation process of textual study or in deep engagement with a congregational member or issue, the focus of the message is God's gracious activity in respect to a particular human situation. In other words, the presence and activity of the crucified and risen Christ in the lives of believers today is the essential "good news."

The "good news," of course, is targeted differently depending on the human situation to be addressed. The good news of forgiveness in Jesus Christ is appropriate for guilty Christians; but for those troubled primarily by anxiety, the good news may be God's peace. For those who feel lonely and isolated, the good news may be community in Christ. If a sense of estrangement is the concern, the emphasis should fall on reconciliation. Following Tillich's principle of correlation, preachers need to find an appropriate relationship between each human dilemma and the gospel. The church is not served and preaching is not helpful unless the theologian or the preacher "moves back and forth between two poles, the eternal truth of [the Christian message] and the temporal situation in which the eternal truth must be received."[6]

In the end, we are going to take a functional approach to pastoral preaching. J. Randall Nichols defines pastoral communication as "human communication which affects and involves the deeply personal in us and, moreover, which does so to some extent by the design and intention of the communicator."[7] Preachers need to be intentional about shaping the message with theological and pastoral content, but finally what makes preaching pastoral is the impact of the sermon on the listener, whether "intended by the preacher or supplied by the hearers."[8] Beyond the particular intent, the sermon may function to heal hurts in the lives of listeners. This functional definition of pastoral preaching helps us to think concretely about its major goals or objectives.

1. *Giving voice to human lament.* Suffering often reduces afflicted ones to silence. Sermons that verbalize feelings, for example, of protest and anger at seemingly unfair and unjust suffering, even anger at God, may serve the pastoral function of assisting sufferers to acknowledge and work through negative feelings. The psalms of lament in the Old Testament have functioned this way for generations of believers.

2. *Assisting listeners to face reality.* Helping persons to make sense of life is a primary goal of pastoral preaching. In part, this is a cognitive function, but a more profound reorientation of the person is envisioned that affects both emotions and will in a hopeful way. Enabling believers to face the reality that they are redeemed sinners and that most human problems are rooted in a continuing rebellion against God's rule in their lives is a crucial step in the process of dealing hopefully with life.

3. *Making suffering endurable.* Hope enables people to endure in the face of profound problems. While rejecting false hopes and facile assurances, the preaching of the gospel enables believers to persist in their living and serving without sinking into despair. The gospel does not erase all suffering and sadness, but it can communicate the love and concern of both God and the Christian community.

4. *Strengthening faith.* In the face of personal problems, faith is not the assurance that everything will turn out all right. As Tillich defines it, faith is "ultimate concern," risking life on God in whom we put our trust. With the total investment of the self, with unreserved commitment, Christians are able to approach struggle knowing that the one in whom we trust is with us and sustains us.

5. *Giving a sense of joy.* Believers can experience joy even in the midst of trouble. This joy, deeper than happiness, is possible for those who live on this side of Easter. As Douglas John Hall reflects, "a Christian community that has undergone the cross and the night has the right to announce the dawn."[9] Preaching is a prime medium for that joyful announcement.

The Form of the Pastoral Sermon

As the form of the pastoral sermon unfolds, it will be clear that its two major components (we term them "movements," as in a symphony) derive from key purposes of the message. Assisting listeners to give voice to human lament while facing the reality of suffering gives rise to the first movement, the Problem of Suffering, while the goal of assisting listeners to have faith strengthened and to know joy in the midst of pain is fulfilled in the second movement, the Response of Faith. Taken together, these two components help believers to endure suffering hopefully without giving in to despair.

We believe that engagement with the biblical text and the human situation of suffering will clarify the purpose of each pastoral sermon and will guide preachers in shaping the message. Rather than sermon forms being vessels of fixed shape into which the content of the message is poured or totally unique to each message, design hints are found in listener needs in a given situation.

Similarly, the smaller components of the sermon (we term them "moments") ought to be determined by their function. For example, the need to assist listeners to feel and express negative feelings (for example, giving voice to human lament) can be accomplished by a biblical text that is candid about human feelings or by a contemporary example(s) that does the same. Faith is often strengthened when a pastoral sermon explicates a theological theme of the faith, which enables perceptive listeners to make sense of suffering. Giving a sense of joy may be accomplished in a variety of ways, including the direct proclamation of the gospel for sufferers.

Movement 1: The Problem of Suffering

In working with any biblical text as part of the exegetical process, the preacher ought to ask, "What human experience of suffering arises out of this text?" Sometimes suffering, replete with human emotions, is prominent in the text. In such cases, the preacher is able to make contact with listeners by relating the biblical narrative in a vivid and dramatic way. However, when suffering and its dynamics are not overt, retelling the biblical story may still be useful to set the scene. This was the case in the sermon preached on the appointed Easter text of John 21:1-19: "Simon Peter said to (the disciples), 'I am going fishing.' They said to him, 'We will go with you.' They went out and got into the boat, but that night they caught nothing."[10]

> Simon and his friends, fishermen by trade, had put in a night's work, but there was nothing to show for it but empty nets. Their livelihood depended upon the water and its creatures. They were used to the fickle tides and currents, the wind and weather. They knew the hiding places where the fish were apt to be found, "but that night they caught nothing."

Images, the mental and imaginary pictures evoked in listeners by language, are critical to communicating with the television generation. Modern humans are visually oriented, and studies indicate that verbal pictures impact the imagination and lodge in the conscious mind. When suffering is not overt in the biblical text, a contemporary picture may move listeners closer to that reality while naming a specific manifestation of suffering. That was the intended function of a personal story in the John 21 sermon.

> I can relate to the frustration of the disciples. Last summer, rising well before the July sun my friend and I pushed off from the dock in our one-day rental and headed across the bay to catch breakfast. The water was flat and still with a layer of mist rolling a foot or so above its surface. As we reached the fishing place, two ducks rose in flight as we invaded their privacy. But as the first rosy glow of dawn appeared and the sky gradually opened to full sun, our sense of anticipation began to fade. No sea creatures arose to break the water's surface. No poles bent with strikes. No reels sang as they emptied themselves of line. Hours later, two frustrated fishermen returned to the dock empty-handed.

Pastorally, for an older declining congregation in a depressed city neighborhood, it seemed important to deepen the human issue by moving from the frustration of the disciples in the text to the more profound experience of the seeming failure of their mission. The disciples were back in Galilee fishing, and Jesus seemed nowhere to be found. Had his ministry ended in failure?

Pastoral preachers regularly ask, "How is this suffering being experienced?" "Has the suffering been named and, if appropriate, defined?" This "moment" provided a transition from yesterday to today, linking text to life, while at the same time naming the suffering.

> Those of you sitting in the pews this morning, those of you who work day in and day out, those of you who struggle just to make ends meet, may feel stomach muscles tighten at the mention of labor without success. The disciples were returning from fishing empty-handed. You know what that's like, don't you?
> But a larger failure haunted these men. Where was Jesus? What had become of the mission they launched together? With the disciples' lives in shambles, what was left for them but to return to their nets? Can you sense their deep frustration? Can you relate to their lack of success? The Lord had disappeared from their lives, and this apparent failure hurt deeply.

When a human experience of suffering has been named, pastoral preachers will wish to ask two further and related questions: "What emotions are being felt?" "What questions are being asked?" We have said that feelings and cognitive thinking are closely related. While current suffering (for example, death and loss) may cause felt thought to dominate logical thought, with the passage of time people seek perspective on instances of distress. Reflecting people's own words is one way to tune listeners to emotional wavelengths.

> Unfortunately, discouragement and failure are common experiences. Whether on the job, at home, or in the life of a congregation, you and I often have little to show for our efforts. Sometimes nothing appears to work. Sometimes nothing we plan makes a difference. Sometimes life is filled with frustration. Don't you find yourself saying . . . "What's the use?" "Why do I keep knocking my head against a stone wall?" "It's hopeless!"

An important but often neglected step in assisting listeners to confront the reality of suffering is direct engagement with the question "How is this suffering related to sin?" Many pastoral sermons skip this critical move. When preachers attempt to leap from an instance of human suffering to a hopeful theological affirmation without crossing the bridge of sin, listeners fall into confusion. Until suffering has been analyzed theologically, the good news of the gospel feels tacked on and essentially irrelevant.

John 21 pictures the frustration of the disciples whose sin, like ours, often manifests itself in a stubborn dependence on human strength linked to a lack of trust in the risen Christ.

> When you and I fail at something repeatedly, frustration grows and focus narrows. Instead of looking outside for help, instead of turning to God, we often become turned in on ourselves. That narrowed vision, that self-centeredness, that lack of trust the church calls sin.

Movement 2: The Response of Faith

In our sermon sample, the linkage of suffering and sin is used as a transition to set up the proclamation of the good news. The biblical preacher will ask, "What is God, Christ, or the Holy Spirit doing or saying in the text that responds to the suffering being experienced?" Is there a word from the Lord in the face of apparent failure?

> Frustration, failure and hopelessness are *not* the final word— not for the disciples and not for you and for me. Suddenly, without warning, Jesus shouted from the shoreline to those in the boat. He asked, "Children, you have no fish, have you?" Immediately their drooping heads raised. The voice was familiar. A spark was beginning to burn inside. Jesus directed, "Cast the net to the right side of the boat."
>
> On the face of it, the suggestion was crazy. The men were dog-tired and the nets were empty. Fruitless hours had been invested already. Yet Peter and his crew sprang to action. They cast the net as Jesus had directed, and suddenly water, once flat and still, began to boil. Where only the honking of birds broke the stillness flapping sea creatures filled nets, strained nets. "They were not able to haul it in because there were so many fish."

The careful pastoral preacher always asks, "How is this good news experienced in the text? What theme of faith conveys the good news?" In some texts, too many theological themes are evident and a choice must be made. In other biblical passages, the good news seems hidden or absent, and the context of the text or the good sense of the preacher is needed to find a "good news" correlation for the specific suffering being addressed.

In John 21 the risen Christ reveals himself to the disciples both in word and in action. Jesus appears on the beach and speaks a word to frustrated fishermen. The catch of fish, a suggestive sign of Jesus' presence and mission, is an instance of grace, a free gift from God. As was the case earlier in linking human self-reliance to self-centeredness and labeling it "sin," so here the preacher takes the opportunity to do a moment of overt teaching by naming and defining "grace." Such teaching moments are critical when many worshipers are biblically and theologically challenged.

> To frustrated fishermen with furrowed faces and knurled hands, this was God's work, God's miracle. "It is the Lord!" they shouted to one another. No other explanation would do. After a fruitless night of labor, the disciples had an amazing catch of fish. And they had a word from the Lord. Jesus' presence and sign was a gift . . . a gift abundant and overflowing, a gift from God. The church labels such gifts—grace.

A related question to that regarding the good news in the biblical text is this: "How is this good news experienced today?" Our sermon sample from the Third Sunday of Easter moves directly to this issue with a moment of direct proclamation.

> You have experienced such grace, and I have, in life's darkest moments when nothing seemed to be working. You have experienced this grace, and I have, when God plucked us from the midst of failure and blessed our efforts with success. You have experienced this grace, and I have, when failure persisted . . . but when, like the disciples on the shore, we were able to share a meal with the crucified and risen one. "This is my body; this is my blood . . . for you."

As we have said, faith is not the assurance that everything will turn out all right. Occasionally it does. But when it does not, the presence of the living Christ in word and sacrament does strengthen faith and give a sense of joy.

The response of faith to the good news, especially when the biblical text provides hints, properly addresses the appropriate action of disciples. The question "What shall I do?" is an explicit or implicit response to the gospel in many biblical texts. Pastors seeking concreteness in their preaching are sometimes advised to picture a back-pew cynic asking about the Good News, "So what?" "What difference does it make (in my life, in my family, in my work, in the life of my congregation, in my world)?"

One dimension of the response of faith is a sense of direction for living in the face of suffering. Patterns of thought and feeling have profound implications for patterns of action. To put it another way, what a community of faith believes ought to assist that community to live faithfully. The text of John 21 was helpful in giving persons experiencing apparent failure in their congregation's mission not a miracle but direction for continuing to move forward in hope.

> Now on the shore, with the meal served and eaten, with the risen One recognized, Jesus addressed Peter directly: "Follow me. Feed my sheep." Centuries later, what are discouraged fishermen to make of this event? We know what Jesus' command meant for Peter, a mission to bring the gospel to his people, the Jews. What does the presence of the risen One in our midst mean for you and for me?
>
> Like Peter, this community of Zion Lutheran Church is responding to God's call to follow Jesus and to feed the sheep. You are disciples in your families and in your daily work. As a congregation, you are seeking to witness in your neighborhood. Though sometimes discouraged, you are hopeful. Though failure seems more apparent than success, you move forward. Though it's impossible to see the future, you trust in the risen Christ.
>
> For believers, the nets will not remain empty. Discouragement and failure will not be the final word. Peter and his friends left the fish to rot in the morning sun as they hurried

off to spread the "good news." That is your commission as well. Follow Jesus. Feed the sheep.

In summary, the form of the sermon ought to be determined by engagement with the biblical text and its message, the human situation, and by the purposes of a particular pastoral sermon. By asking and answering key questions, the preacher will shape messages that enable listeners to face the reality of suffering while at the same time having faith strengthened and hope renewed. This pattern will be apparent in the topical chapters that follow.

5

Preaching to Believers
Who Experience Loss

Five-year-old Barry was dressed in his new clothes—a pair of blue trousers and a matching short-sleeved shirt. It was his first day of kindergarten. He had attended a preschool nursery the preceding year, but somehow this day seemed different. Something was changing, though he did not have the words to articulate the change. He just felt like crying. His mother said good-bye to him like he was now supposed to be a grown-up little boy. The big bus came, and he had to find a seat among strange faces. He was all alone and did not have his mother to hold him.

A different and much more radical loss was experienced by Job. One day he had many possessions; the next day he suffered greatly at the hands of Satan. His oxen and donkeys were killed when the Sabeans fell upon them and slew the servants who were present. Then a fire fell "from heaven and burned up the sheep and the servants, and consumed them" (Job 1:16). The Chaldeans took his camels and slew those servants. Stripped of all possessions, he then learned that a great wind had buried his sons and daughters under the rubble of his eldest brother's house. To complete the reign of tribulation, Job was afflicted with "loathsome sores . . . from the sole of his foot to the crown of his head" (Job 2:7).

It was obvious, even to Job's three friends, that Job was in intense suffering. His scorched life silenced them. They sat with him for seven days and did not speak a word.

Loss is a terrible experience. It can shatter our world and render us helpless. It can literally knock the props out from under us, because the very thing on which we build our world has suddenly disappeared. When Jesus was attacked by the Pharisees and scribes for eating with sinners, he employed three parables about loss—the lost sheep, the lost coin, and the lost son—to express the joy of getting beyond the ravages of loss (Luke 15).

Actually, loss can come in different forms with different degrees of intensity. At one end of the continuum, it is often a part of our everyday world, experienced in mundane moments like saying good-bye to our children as they go off to school or feeling the pain of being separated from our spouse for the day. At the other end of the continuum, loss can be a complex and intense experience, epitomized in the crash of a commercial airline or the act of a terrorist or the spiteful divorce of a lifelong partner.

To make our discussion of loss more manageable, we are tempted to try to take steps to domesticate it. But in some real sense, what we need to do is to present loss in its raw detail and concrete richness. Only then do we have a realistic notion of what can be done about it, that is, how pastoral preaching should approach it.

A Concrete Instance of Grief

To deal with grief concretely we need to deal with an actual instance of it. Two possibilities come to mind: C. S. Lewis, *A Grief Observed*, and Nicholas Wolterstorff, *Lament for a Son*.[1] Because Wolterstorff's study is a detailed experiential struggle with grief, it will serve our purpose better.

Nicholas Wolterstorff, professor of philosophy at Calvin College in Grand Rapids, Michigan, lost his twenty-five-year-old son, Eric, to a mountain-climbing accident on June 11, 1983. Eric was in Austria for the year doing research for his doctoral dissertation on the beginnings of modern architecture. "He had finished his research and was ready to write."[2] He decided to spend the sun-drenched Saturday climbing alone on a snowy slope in the Kaisergebirger. Around mid-afternoon Michigan time, the phone rang at the Wolterstorff home, and Wolterstorff himself answered it. After making sure that the person who answered was indeed Eric's father, the voice on the other end announced, "Eric has had a serious accident." The voice paused momentarily and then said, "Mr. Wolterstorff, I must tell you, Eric is dead. . . .You must come at once. Mr. Wolterstorff, Eric is dead."[3] A "cold burning pain" ran through the father's body and was followed by an extended struggle with intense grief.

Wolterstorff's grief revolved around the realization that Eric is gone. "It's the *neverness* that is so painful. *Never again* to be here with us—never to sit with us at table, never to travel with us, never to laugh with us, never to cry with us, never to embrace us as he leaves for school, never to see his brothers and sister marry."[4] Death's finality, its foreverness on the earthly side of life, was unrelenting. Not even the attempt to turn back the clock to a time before Eric died brought relief. And when Wolterstorff struggled with the question "Why did Eric climb?" he was only led back to what made Eric irreplaceable: "His deepest self drew him there." Climbing for Eric was an encounter with the "awesome sublimity of the mountains. . . . To go into the mountains was to face God."[5]

As Wolterstorff reclaimed the mutilated body, he saw Eric "bumping, scraping, crashing down the mountain, grasping for a hold, missing, knowing he was to die."[6] Later Wolterstorff struggled with tears or, more precisely, with the cultural mandate that says that men should be strong and not cry. But he could not put a Band-Aid over the wound, the grievous wound, and he looked at the world through eyes filled with tears. He was tempted to try to forget, to gain control by canceling out Eric's death, but instead he decided to remember. "If Eric's life was a gift, surely then we are to hold it in remembrance—to resist amnesia, to renounce oblivion."[7] Besides, Wolterstorff was surrounded by Eric's belongings, "his clothes, his books, his camera, the things he made," and they were a constant reminder of his loss. Eric, his son, was at the peak of his vitality and full of promise—and now he was gone.

Nothing filled the void. Wolterstorff does not put his reflections in a time frame, so we do not know how long he struggled with specific reactions. We only know the intensity of the moment. We only get a sense of grief's progression by the movement from one struggle to the next. His entry about the void occurs just before the funeral. He now lives in a world with a hole in it. "In the place where he was, there's now just nothing. . . . Only a gap remains."[8] The funeral and burial provide a time of leave-taking, but they do not stop the grief. In some sense, they intensify it. "Something is *over*. In the deepest levels of my existence something is finished, done. . . . Especially in places where he and I were together this sense of something *being over* washes over me."[9] Wolterstorff describes the result as "a place of cold inky darkness." His memories of Eric do not lead to life but to an end. "The book slams shut. . . . The future closes, the hopes get crushed. . . . It's all over, over, over."[10]

Shortly after the blackness, there is a glimmer of light. Wolterstorff starts to carry Eric's boxes of books and clothes from the entry to the garage. In the process he hears Eric's "cheerful voice, loud and clear, calling from the entry, 'Hey Dad, I'm back.' "[11] Wolterstorff experienced other moments of relief, but even his assurances of faith, like his belief in the hope of the resurrection, often lead him back to the realities of his loss. "Back and forth, lament and faith, faith and lament, each fastened to the other."[12] In the midst of blackness, he finds that his "faith is not dead," but then his grief returns, and again he laments, "God, my rock, 'Why have you forgotten me?' " (Ps. 42:9).

This is the struggle that must be addressed by our pastoral ministry and by our pastoral preaching. But before we get to that, we must pinpoint the issues and dynamics that are involved in Wolterstorff's grief. As he himself says, all grievers grieve differently. "As each death has its own character, so too each grief over a death has its own character—its own inscape."[13] But there are also many commonalities, many things that grievers share given their common plight. Our primary concern now is to explicate Wolterstorff's grief from the perspective of pastoral ministry.

The Pastoral Issues of Loss

Wolterstorff is dealing with an untimely death, a death that is thoroughly out of line with the usual course of events. "The burial of one's child is a wrenching alteration of expectations."[14] But Wolterstorff knew that there was something more involved. There was the lifelong attempt to protect and to nurture a child and with it the delights of seeing the child's future begin to unfold and take shape. Then the unexpected happened. The future that Wolterstorff had begun to embrace was destroyed. Eric "slipped out of my arms," and the whole world seemed out of joint. This time warp caused Wolterstorff to return again and again to struggle with the unbelievable realization that Eric was gone. In other cases where death is more timely, like the death of an ailing grandparent, the sense of loss may be less intense or may even be disarmed by the feeling that the death was a blessing.

Wolterstorff is also dealing with a sudden death, one that comes out of the blue and gives him no time to prepare. In other words, Wolterstorff did not have the cushion of anticipated grief. Instead, one moment Eric was alive, the next he was gone. Anticipatory grief does not take away all the blows of grief and, in fact, it may carry blows of its own as the mourners swing between hope and hopelessness. But it does force the mourners to deal with the possibility of loss or at least with the denial of such a possibility. On that fateful Saturday afternoon, the shadow of Eric's dying had probably never darkened Wolterstorff's mind. When the news came, the shock was dramatic and the need to say a final good-bye was never satisfied. Wolterstorff could only touch "him in his coffin"[15] and take leave of him.

Wolterstorff highlights another aspect of grief—the finality of death or, as he says, the neverness of death. Often not even anticipatory grief helps us to deal with death as an irrevocable termination. It is only after death has occurred that we are fully aware of death's foreverness. Wolterstorff gives extended and dramatic expression to this aspect of grief, relatively, by observing that now he can only remember Eric and not experience him; absolutely by realizing that Eric is gone and that what he was meant to be will never be.

Pastoral ministry must help the mourner to deal with death's finality, and it can do that least of all by a hurried reassurance that there is life after death. Wolterstorff found that "elements of the gospel which I had always thought would console did not."[16] To be reminded of the resurrection was one of those elements. Wolterstorff grants that if he had forgotten that hope, a reminder of it may "have brought light into my life," but he was struggling at a different point—with the raw reality that "Eric is gone, *here and now* he is gone."[17] For Wolterstorff, there is no consolation for that except "having him back."

Wolterstorff has an important pastoral lesson to teach us. Before we can find comfort in faith's affirmation that death is not a final end but a new beginning, we are going to have to take seriously his longing to have Eric back. "To comfort me, you have to come close. Come sit beside me on the mourning bench."[18] If we join Wolterstorff, maybe not physically but certainly humanly, we will journey with him as he struggles with other facets of grief: the isolation of grief because each person grieves differently; the regrets of grief because of what was done or not done for the deceased; the acute pain of grief on special holidays; and most of all the emptiness of grief because life has lost its zest and ordinary activities have lost their importance. In the process it is our empathic presence, and not our specific words, that will console: "Your words don't have to be wise. The heart that speaks is heard more than the words spoken."[19]

Wolterstorff's loss sent him on a prolonged struggle with God. His struggle was not that God was the agent of Eric's death, that is, that God predetermines when and how we are to die. He was convinced that God "is appalled by death" and seeks to overcome it. Neither does he buy into Rabbi Kushner's belief that though God is pained by death, God is not able to do anything about it. Wolterstorff struggles with God at a different point. He could not fit together his belief in "God the Father Almighty, maker of heaven and earth and resurrecter of Jesus Christ" and his belief that his "son's life was cut off in its prime."[20] He had no answer for why God, who is for life, would stand by as a loved one is critically wounded. "I do not know why God would watch him fall. I do not know why God would watch me wounded. I cannot even guess."[21] Baffled and hurt, he confesses, "My wound is an unanswered question. . . . I can do nothing else than endure in the face of this deepest and most painful of mysteries."[22]

Wolterstorff's grief reminds us of how confused mourners can be about where God is in suffering. We certainly should try to find out. We must also attend to the emotional component of their confusion. Wolterstorff was baffled and hurt. That requires a different pastoral response than if he had been angry and rebellious. Both responses may come from what Wolterstorff calls a darkness, but how the mourner dwells in that darkness determines the tone and direction of our pastoral response. Wolterstorff approaches the situation as an anxious and distraught inquirer: "Will my eyes adjust to this darkness? Will I find you [God] in the dark—not in the streaks of light which remain, but in the darkness? Has anyone ever found you there? Did they love what they saw?"[23]

Underneath Wolterstorff's words looms the threat of despair. But this moment also seems to be a turning point in his grief. He begins to struggle directly with the reality and mystery of human suffering, and in the process he is led to a God who suffers. "Through the prism of my tears I have seen a suffering God." Wolterstorff finds not only a God who shares our suffering but also a God whose very nature is suffering. "God is Love. That is why he suffers."[24] "Every act of evil extracts a tear from God, every plunge into anguish extracts a sob from God."[25] And in the midst of this sorrow God promises the mourner that a day of peace is coming, a day when "those who mourn . . . shall be comforted."

A dramatic turn has taken place. Wolterstorff moves from a God who is absent, or at least is an enigma, in suffering to a God whose very being is concerned about those who suffer. The turn is not a once-for-all event. Wolterstorff is not done with his grief, but God is seen in a different light and a certain amount of peace is experienced. And yet a year after Eric's burial, Wolterstorff visited his grave and wondered how "it will be when God raises [Eric] and the rest of us from the dead."[26] The resurrection of our bodies is not a problem for Wolterstorff, but the viability of the communion of saints is. "How is [God] going to fit us all together into his city?"[27] To paraphrase Wolterstorff: "How is Eric, a man of the twentieth century, going to relate to someone who lived long ago in a nontechnical world?" This seems like a strange question coming from a grieving father, and yet it is a concern about relationships, about how Wolterstorff will experience his son in the hereafter. "Will I hear Eric say someday, *really* now I mean, 'Hey Dad, I'm back'? "[28] This is not a question of "if " but a question of identity. "Will I recognize Eric in the hereafter, and will we still have a special relationship?" Because Wolterstorff can rest in the power of God over death, he ends his lament for a son by saying good-bye to him until they see what God has in store for them.

The *Lament* of Wolterstorff, born out of an intense struggle with loss and involving a forthright struggle with God, is instructive for our pastoral ministry. It tells us that the pastoral task is not easy and that there may never be a permanent closure to the mourner's grief. But it also tells us that there are powerful resources that are available to the believer: the love of those who care, the understanding of those who sit on the mourner's bench with us, the memories we have of the deceased, the courage that we are given to face death honestly, the faith in a power beyond ourselves, and above all, the presence and the promise of a God who himself has suffered. In all of this, our pastoral ministry must remember what Wolterstorff himself discovered: "Not even the best of words can take away the pain. What words can do is to testify that there is more than pain in our journey on earth to a new day."[29] The "more" may vary with each person, and it is the task of pastoral ministry to discover what that is. But for the believer its anchor point is that, in spite of all appearances, God is with us, even in our darkest moments. This truth is not to be proclaimed as a dogmatic fact. God does not come to us or comfort us as doctrine but as a concrete and incarnated reality. God is found in the preached Word or in the fellowship of the Eucharist or in the touch of a concerned friend. God comes to us enfleshed in human relationships.

In our discussion of Wolterstorff's loss, we have considered it from the pastoral ministry point of view. Pastoral ministry is a broad ministry of care that uses the resources of Word, sacrament, visitation, and other activities to address the mourner in a variety of situations. Pastoral care, a specialized form of pastoral ministry, would focus on specific aspects of Wolterstorff's grief and would help him to struggle with them on a personal basis. Our central concern, though, is with pastoral preaching. How is the pastor in the pulpit to relate to Wolterstorff and to speak God's Word of comfort to him? We now turn to this question.

Preaching to Wolterstorff

In preparing to preach to Wolterstorff, the pastoral preacher must go through a diagnostic process, whether it is conscious or not. He or she must be mindful of the dynamics that are characteristic of the type of death being confronted while at the same time being attentive to how this particular instance of suffering is being experienced. Eric Wolterstorff's death was both untimely and sudden,[30] providing no opportunity for his father (family) and friends to say good-bye. This fact may complicate Wolterstorff's grief and add an important concern to the content of the pastoral sermon.

In the diagnostic process, conversation with a survivor or a number of survivors is critical. The pastor needs to listen actively as the story of the loss is shared. If the death was sudden, as in Wolterstorff's case, the narrative may be confused and halting, interrupted by emotional outbursts and tortured questions. This means that the pastor may find himself or herself moving between giving pastoral care and formulating a picture of the father's (family's) grief.

The pastor should be especially alert to the emotions that are being felt by the mourners. Shock and disbelief engulfed Eric's father. As might be expected, his grief came in waves, leaving him disoriented and confused. He described it as being immersed in darkness and alone in a void, which sometimes bordered on despair. Often, anger comes with an accidental death, but since Eric died alone, there was no reckless driver or careless friend to blame. Thus Wolterstorff was more hurt and confused than angry.

Initially, Wolterstorff may have blamed his son for undertaking the solitary climb, but quickly the focus of the father's hurt shifted to God ("God, my rock, 'Why have you forgotten me?' "). He struggled with God's fairness (a life was "cut off in its prime") and God's abandonment ("Will I find you in the dark?"). These are difficult issues, but in the midst of grief's devastation, mourners search for answers that deal with the basic concerns of life. "Funerals are, of course, a time to reflect on your life. I mean, if you need any evidence that you're not immortal, that hole in the ground is it. So you naturally start to wonder if you're getting it right, then you wonder why it matters if you do."[31]

Finally, the preacher should pay special attention to the images of loss and grief that are used by the mourners. Since mourners feel more than they reason, the images they use may be very descriptive of their struggle. Wolterstorff spoke of Eric's death in terms of a book slamming shut as a way to express the fact that something in his life is over, is gone forever. He also used repeatedly the image of darkness to describe grief's void where God's presence or care is not at all apparent. Pastoral preaching must take these images seriously and address the struggle behind them. It must witness to the light in the midst of darkness. It must point to hope where there seems to be no hope. It must proclaim new life when death seems to reign supreme.

When the pastor has completed the diagnostic process, the first movement of Eric's funeral sermon can be formed. The movement should help mourners face the reality of Eric's death

- by retelling the story of death
- by identifying the emotions being felt and by posing the theological questions being asked
- by focusing on images of loss and grief that spark imagination and touch feelings

In all of this, the content of the sermon emerges from and is directed to a particular loss. No canned funeral sermon will do, for listeners quickly spot the dog-eared notes and generic messages that bear a "to whom it may concern" label. In response to Eric's death and Wolterstorff's grief, the question is, "What is God's good news for this situation? In the face of concerns about death's finality ("never again") and God's apparent abandonment, what biblical text or texts will convey the good news?" These questions lead into the second movement, which deals with the response of faith to loss.

Typically, the choice of a biblical text is left to the discretion of the preacher. Sometimes a favorite text of the dead person or of the family is suggested to the pastor. If that text does not convey adequately an appropriate theme of faith, the lesson simply can be read as part of the liturgy. It need not become the preaching text. The question to be posed to any potential biblical text is, "What is God doing here, first of all in this text, then in response to this situation of death and loss?"

For Eric's funeral, a number of passages suggest themselves for possible use. While pictures of family reunions in heaven rarely strike a resonant cord with mourners, passages replete with images of light may begin to address the dark feelings and thoughts of this grieving father.

- Revelation 21:1-4. In the new Jerusalem, where death and grief are overcome, the glory of God and the Lamb give light. "And there will be no night there."
- John 1:1-5. Jesus, the Word of God, overcomes darkness, giving light and life.
- John 8:12. Jesus, the Light of the World, brightens the daily walk of believers.

These passages and others like them should be related to the main elements of Wolterstorff's grief, namely, to the absence of his son and the apparent abandonment by God, knowing that these feelings may be exacerbated by the suddenness of Eric's death, which left no chance to say goodbye. That is the stark reality of Wolterstorff's loss, but the sermon should also include a ray of light. The pastoral preacher must affirm, intellectually and emotionally, that the loved one is in God's care. Eric's baptism, and his apparent steadfastness in the faith, can provide the needed basis for this reassurance. And the use of commendatory prayers at the end of many funeral liturgies today enable mourners like Wolterstorff to say good-bye even as he gives his lost loved one over to God. This "giving over" encourages a positive relationship with the dead person in and through the mystical body of Christ.

In the early centuries of Christian history, funeral prayers often included petitions commending the dead person into the restful arms of God (and the patriarchs). Frequently themes of rest and waiting were linked to those of peace and blessing. Petitions for safe conduct to heaven and protection by angels on the perilous journey were also common. As the centuries passed, these formulas were scarred by an increasing emphasis on sin and guilt and thus on the need for absolution. Wisely, many contemporary liturgies have muted the note of absolution without eliminating it in order to highlight the commendation.

> Into your hands, O merciful Savior, we commend your servant N. Acknowledge, we humbly beseech you, a sheep of your own fold, a lamb of your own flock, a sinner of your own redeeming. Receive him/her into the arms of your mercy, into the blessed rest of everlasting peace, and into the glorious company of the saints in light.[32]

In sermon preparation, the words of the commendation may be a sufficient text for preaching. If so, leave-taking will be both spoken about in the sermon and enacted at the conclusion of the liturgy. The commendation also includes images of God as shepherd and of believers as part of the flock, so that God's ongoing care is announced. This theme is prevalent in two passages that are often used as preaching texts.

- Psalm 23: The Lord as shepherd leads the sheep through the darkest valleys to pleasant pastures, comforting them.
- John 10:11-15: Jesus, the good shepherd, lays down his life for the sheep.

The passage from John may be especially appropriate for Wolterstorff, because it speaks about a God of love who suffers. It was this God who finally gave a measure of peace to Wolterstorff.

With ample gospel resources in hand, the pastoral preacher is ready to prepare the second and final movement of Eric's funeral sermon.

The movement, dealing primarily with the response of faith, should assist the mourners to discover the hope of new life in Christ

- by utilizing a biblical passage to convey a comforting vision of God to suffering believers
- by projecting images and themes of hope and healing
- by assisting mourners to envision new life in Christ for the lost one and for themselves

Preaching to Loss Generally

When we move from radical losses like death and the response of funeral preaching to more general preaching about loss, it is important to note that many of the same steps are involved in both the diagnosis of the loss and the preparation of the sermon.

Briefly, the preacher begins with the problem of loss and its dynamics. This is true whether the loss is personal (for example, aging, with a potential loss of vitality and meaning), congregational (for example, decline of a congregation in size and vitality), community (for example, a key plant closure with loss of jobs), or societal (for example, the passage of a way of life). As part of the diagnostic process, the preacher reflects about what people are feeling, what theological questions are being asked, and what images of loss may be useful in preaching.

For instance, in the novel *The Gold Coast*, the principal characters are struggling with the decline and immanent death of a way of life. Part of the enduring worth of this fine novel, in addition to its strong characterizations, is Nelson DeMille's ability to articulate both feelings and implicit questions using vivid imagery.

> I know that we are fighting a rearguard action here to protect a way of life that should have ended twenty or thirty years ago. I understand this, and I'm not bitter. I'm just amazed that we've gotten away with it this long. In that respect I say God Bless America, land of evolution and not revolution.[33]

With the specific problems of loss diagnosed, the preacher seeks a clear understanding of God's good news. The preacher asks again and again questions like: What is God doing here? Where is hope to be found? What biblical texts contain theological themes to address this loss? What images in the Bible, in literature, or in life can be employed to make hope vivid and memorable for listeners? Answers to these questions will help the pastor formulate a sermon that is truly pastoral.

Finding Hope in the Midst of Loss

Mourners live by hope even as they experience loss as an instance of hopelessness. The pastoral preacher has various resources to help mourners live in hope.

In the Old Testament the term *death* is often "used as a metaphor for those things which hinder full life."[34] It is used in the book of Ezekiel to describe the exilic community, imprisoned and demoralized in Babylon. The Word of the Lord comes to the valley of dry bones and brings them back to life. The graves open up, and the people are brought home to the land of Israel (see Ezekiel 37). These images of bleached bones and open graves can speak volumes to persons whose suffering has left them imprisoned or decimated.

In the fourth Gospel, death becomes a metaphor for the type of existence that the followers of Jesus have transcended. Though they die biologically, Jesus' followers do not participate in an existence that is oriented toward death. The presence of the suffering and risen Lord gives life to believers beginning in the present age. Those who hear the word of Jesus and believe have already passed from death to life (see John 5:24). And in raising Lazarus from death, Jesus proclaims that, for believers, he is the key to both resurrection from death and new life in the present (see John 11:1-27).

The contemporary rediscovery of baptism, with its connection between Jesus' death and resurrection and new life, is also a source of hope. Using a variety of words and signs, the first Christians proclaimed that death to sin has already occurred in baptism and that the despair of physical death and loss is qualified and eased for those who are washed and sealed. Believers are initiated into the community of the end time where sin and death are overcome daily (see Rom. 6:1-11). Life remains a struggle, but in the risen

Christ, in his body the church, believers already begin to experience new life.

The pall, placed over the casket at the entrance of the church, is a stylized form of the basic baptismal garment. To the initiated, such a symbol suggests a robe of righteousness, a garment of victory.

> A pall may be placed upon the coffin by the pallbearers or other assisting ministers, and the following may be said. (P) When we were baptized in Christ Jesus, we were baptized into his death. We were buried therefore with him by Baptism into death, so that as Christ was raised from the dead by the glory of the Father, we too might live a new life. For if we have been united with him in a death like his, we shall certainly be united with him in a resurrection like his.[35]

As Paul makes clear, behind baptism stands the crucified Christ, who witnesses to the real source of our comfort and hope, namely, a suffering God. It is only a God of suffering who can minister to us in our suffering. Indeed, the One who gave up the only Son to suffering turns to suffering believers before they turn to God (see Luke 15). Through Word and Sacrament, God offers support and comfort for lonely and anxious believers, inviting them to turn to the divine presence, even as in their darkness the Healer turns to them.

The efficacy of the crucified God is often ambiguous in the midst of traumatic loss. Suffering believers walk by faith, not by inerrant sight or, as Paul says, "now we see in a mirror, dimly . . . Now [we] know only in part" (1 Cor. 13:12). The comfort of baptism is that God acts to accept us as his own, even when we in our grief have turned away from God or even have turned against our source of hope.

Conclusion

Persons and communities who have experienced any kind of loss have a desperate need to find meaning in life. When a relationship is broken or a valued possession destroyed, life suddenly seems empty and devoid of meaning. Pastoral preachers help listeners to face the reality of loss as the first step toward healing.

Pastoral preachers also point beyond loss to a God who is for life, not just for new life after death but for new life that begins now in the waters of baptism. They proclaim Christ crucified, for this Christ is a man of sorrows who is acquainted with loss. He is able and willing to travel with us through the dark recesses of grief and to bring healing to our sorrowing spirit.

6

Preaching to Believers Who Are Ill

Joseph Knight enjoyed good health until he was fifty-three. Then his shortness of breath was diagnosed as emphysema, and his lifelong struggle to quit smoking suddenly became much easier. But it was too late. Joe became progressively worse until he died at seventy-eight. Friends were surprised by how long he lived. He experienced the time as twenty-five years of progressive pain and panic.

Joe was a strong man who prided himself on putting in a full day's work. His job as a construction worker demanded it, and his livelihood depended on it. He was the sole support of his family of four, and that gave him a certain amount of needed authority.

Joe first noticed a change in his health when he felt tired and washed out after a regular day's work. When work demanded more effort, he was aware that his heart throbbed in his chest as he struggled for air. He wondered why the flu kept hanging on. He decided to see his physician when an older friend with similar symptoms was diagnosed with heart trouble.

The doctor's announcement came as a surprise. A friend who had emphysema flashed in his mind, and the full force of the bitter news swept over him. He could see his friend gasping for air and struggling for strength. It was not a pretty picture. What he did not fully anticipate were the times when he would feel helpless, the times when he would feel caught in the clutches of a monster he could not escape.

Though paradigmatic in its own right, Joe's condition represents only one instance of illness. Illness takes many different forms with various degrees of intensity under all kinds of circumstances. We are not interested in providing an all-inclusive definition of illness versus health. Instead, we are interested in the experiential side of illness, in what illness means to the person who has it. After all, it is the person's reaction to, or experience of, illness that is of primary concern to pastoral preaching.

Illness as a Personal Experience

Being ill is an individual experience, yet it has experiential dimensions to it that are shared by most patients. We need to get acquainted with these dimensions, for they clarify the existential state of believers who are ill and can be used as diagnostic tools to determine the needs of particular individuals.

Illness as Discomfort

Joe first noticed his illness because of the discomfort it caused him. He was physically uncomfortable, and his uncomfortableness increased as he engaged in certain activities, sometimes to the point where he could not ignore it. The discomfort did not necessarily indicate what was wrong, but it was a good indication that something was not right and needed attention. In some cases, discomfort is not a dependable barometer of illness. Certain illnesses like cancer and heart trouble do not cause immediate discomfort, so the person can be diseased without knowing it.

Joe's physical discomfort had a mental or emotional component, which is to say that often illness is a systemic condition and not just a localized happening. A headache, or even a splinter in the finger, affects the functioning of the whole person. The individual is more or less preoccupied with, or even handicapped by, the illness until it is taken care of.

Discomfort describes a mild reaction to illness. Many illnesses, including Joe's, induce a reaction on the other end of the continuum—that is, they induce significant suffering or even bring intolerable pain. Where the individual is located on this continuum is important to the pastoral preacher, because that determines what the patient needs and how the patient may respond to what is said. In the early stages of Joe's illness, he was available to interpersonal interaction and enjoyed casual conversation; in the later stages of his illness, he was much more withdrawn and was only concerned about his moment-to-moment survival.

Illness as Judgment

In chapter 1 we dealt with the biblical, especially the Old Testament, idea that God rewards the righteous and punishes the wicked. This retributive understanding of God did not hold up to the experience of people back there, and it does not hold up to our experience. Yet people today continue to see God in that way. In fact, when people become ill, one of their first reactions is to see their illness as a punishment from God.

Joe struggled with this thought. At the beginning of his illness, he asked his pastor what he had done to deserve emphysema. When the pastor denied any connection between Joe's goodness and his illness, Joe dismissed further discussion of the thought by saying, "God can act like human beings at times, can't he?" As Joe's illness progressed, his struggle with a retributive God progressed. Instead of seeing his illness as an act of judgment for particular misdeeds, he struggled with the feeling that his illness was a sign of God's outright condemnation of him. He felt that God had forsaken him, because God did not think that he deserved anything better. Joe's reaction to being forsaken was to forsake God and to feel very sorry for himself. Joe died in this state, though at times he could grant that God had been with him and had gotten him through some tough times.

Illness seen as judgment or as condemnation is a central concern to pastoral preaching. The pastor who sees this struggle in a parishioner may have to address it in a one-to-one relationship, but the issue also needs to be addressed from the pulpit, not necessarily when it puts the spotlight on a particular person but when it is an issue of general concern.

Illness as Loss

One of the primary ways in which illness is experienced is as loss. That is not surprising, for illness, whether acute or chronic, often involves significant loss—the loss of a job due to the patient's inability to perform it; the loss of family and friends as they distance themselves from the suffering of the patient; the loss of self-control as the disease, or even the hospital stay, curtails daily activities, discourages proactive decision-making, and takes away autonomy over the body. The threatened loss of one's future, occasioned by the presence of a terminal illness, is of course the ultimate loss.

Joe's situation was a series of losses spread over twenty-five years with daily ups and downs. One day his breathing was good; the next day the humidity was high and his breathing was labored. One week Joe could keep up with his son as the two of them worked around the house; the next week Joe had to take frequent breaks. Near the end of his illness, Joe fared tolerably well at night on an oxygen tank; the next day or week he landed in the hospital, stricken by panic in his attempts to get enough air.

As we have seen in the previous chapter, loss brings with it grief. So along with the many other concerns with which the patient must struggle, there is grief, sometimes prolonged and profound grief. If the patient's grief becomes excessive or begins to erode the patient's self-esteem, it can turn into depression, into a state of despair with no apparent way out.

In any case, illness is experienced as loss, and in some cases we are talking about an irretrievable loss, for example, when an uncontrolled case of diabetes leads to the loss of limb or sight.

Illness as Loneliness

As people withdraw from the patient, illness can become a lonely experience. In fact, whether people withdraw or not, illness is an experience of loneliness, because it sets the person apart from the healthy people around him or her.

Loneliness comes in different colors, ranging from the pastel experience of being temporarily separated from a loved one to the black experience of utter isolation, during which everyone seems distant and unconcerned.

Joe was not a particularly social creature when he was healthy. He enjoyed an evening with friends, but he also needed his private time. He was not prepared for the loneliness that came with his illness. The problem was not that friends shunned him because they thought he had some contagious disease. Nor did they avoid him because they were impatient with his slow movements and limited activity. Instead of shunning him, they related to him as though he had some pathetic disease. They pitied him or, if they moved beyond that response, they treated him like a child who needed help. That set him apart and isolated him not only from his friends but also from his own resources of strength. He was lonely in his illness, and his illness made it increasingly difficult for him to reach out to others.

Illness as Uncertain Future

Illness, especially if its exact nature is undiagnosed, is a state of not knowing what lies ahead. And if the illness is terminal, it threatens a state of no future at all. Illness does not have to be this extreme, however, to represent a situation in which the person is not at all sure what is around the next corner. Almost any illness has its unexpected turns, and many remedies can have their unpredictable consequences. Sherwin B. Nuland's study *How We Die* is a graphic portrayal of how one thing leads to another, specifically how one condition has a deleterious effect on the rest of the system. As an example, Nuland observes that malnutrition results in more than just weight loss and exhaustion. If the person has cancer, the body uses protein instead of fat as its "main energy source." This decrease in protein, especially if it is aggravated by "lessened food intake," causes "muscle wasting," but even more important it "contributes to the dysfunction of organs and enzyme systems and may significantly affect the immune response" and thereby increase the patient's "susceptibility to infection."[1] Any serious illness threatens to lead the patient "down the dusty road," and most patients are not sure they want to go where the road may take them.

Joe's struggle for oxygen painted a visible picture of an uncertain future on his body. He started off as a muscular, robust man weighing 180 pounds. He ended up as a thin, almost fragile, man who tipped the scales with his clothes on at 116. The loss of weight was gradual, but nevertheless the message that the future was questionable became increasingly evident to those around him, if not to Joe himself. In some cases of illness, of course, the message of uncertainty may be far less evident, but still being ill is itself a portend of an uncertain future.

In summary, then, Joe experienced his illness in many different ways, for example, as guilt, grief, and uncertainty. The importance of each one of these experiences cannot be minimized, for each experience, or all of them put together, is a fitting object of our pastoral preaching when we are dealing with parishioners who are struggling with illness or when the congregation as a whole is struggling with the illness of a beloved member. But these experiences, however distressing or profound, do not exhaust our pastoral concern for believers who are involved with illness. Illness, if it is serious at all, induces yet another struggle. We will call it the struggle with anxiety. In some respects, this struggle is in addition to the five we have already mentioned. In other respects, it is a deeper dimension, or a further extension, of all five. In any case, it is of central importance to our pastoral preaching.

The Pastoral Importance of Anxiety

Of anxiety, Paul Tillich says, "It is impossible for a finite being to stand naked anxiety for more than a flash of time. People who have experienced these moments, as for instance some mystics in their visions of the 'night of the soul,' or Luther under the despair of the demonic assaults, or Nietzsche-Zarathustra in the experience of the 'great disgust,' have told of the unimaginable horror of it."[2] What this means in terms of parishioners is that the pastor will seldom see a person in the throes of anxiety. Parishioners may refer to panic attacks or talk about moments of being frightened to death, but unless we are aware of the thrust of these statements, we will not fathom the depth of their terror. They themselves may be relatively unaware of it. In fact, because anxiety is so terrifying, parishioners often do whatever it takes to silence it. Only in unguarded moments are they seized by it and wake up to find themselves in a cold sweat.

Joe experienced anxiety most often as a vague threat. He felt that something was lurking around the corner, but he seldom identified it as his inability to breathe. Sometimes at night, as he was on the verge of going to sleep, the threat became uglier. He would be jerked back to full consciousness, aware that his heart was pounding and his chest was heaving. Joe had a great urge to get out of there, but there was really no place to go. Gradually, slowly his sense of helplessness would ease, and he would stare at the ceiling until he fell asleep.

Anxiety does not need to occur in its raw form to be of concern to the pastoral preacher. Paul Tillich helps us to understand the basic import of anxiety.[3] He maintains that we can experience anxiety in three different spheres of our life. First, there is moral anxiety. /,
We experience moral anxiety when we violate our own best interests. According to Tillich, we are not only given life, but we also hold ourselves accountable for what we have made of it. Since all of us fall

short of what we could be, we experience moral anxiety, relatively, in the form of guilt; absolutely, in the form of condemnation. Second, there is spiritual anxiety. Tillich sees us as centered creatures, as creatures who must participate in and be a part of a world beyond ourselves. When we lose that centeredness, maybe by being immersed in penultimate realities but certainly when we fall away from an ultimate relationship, we experience spiritual anxiety: relatively, in terms of emptiness; absolutely, in terms of meaninglessness. Finally, there is what Tillich calls ontic anxiety, which is precipitated by a threat that endangers our very existence. There is no ultimate necessity for our lives. In fact, uncontrollable and even unpredictable forces can wipe us out in a split second. When we become aware of our contingent status, whatever the reason, we experience ontic anxiety, the dread of not existing at all.

Illness, whether mental or physical, can cause anxiety in any one of these three spheres. If illness threatens our fulfillment or especially if we perceive it as a judgment on our lives, we experience moral anxiety. Likewise, if illness diminishes our participation in meaningful relationships or enterprises, and especially if it separates us from whatever gives ultimate meaning to our lives, we experience spiritual anxiety. Finally, if our very existence is threatened, either by immediate forces or by distant possibilities, we experience ontic anxiety. While each of these anxieties can be a part of our struggle with illness, it is the third type of anxiety—ontic anxiety—that is basic to, and active in, acute or chronic illness.

Joe's illness represented a threat to his very existence. Ironically, the threat was embodied in the nature of his illness. Emphysema robbed him of his breath, the very thing that is said to give humans life in the creation story (see Gen. 2:7) and the very thing that is impeded in the constrictive affect of anxiety. Nuland makes it clear how critical an adequate supply of oxygen is and how drastic a deprivation of oxygen becomes.

> It takes a great deal of energy to keep the brain's engine functioning efficiently. Almost all of that energy is derived by the tissue's ability to break down glucose into its component parts of carbon dioxide and water, a biochemical process that requires a high level of oxygen. The brain does not have the capacity to keep any glucose in reserve; it depends on a constant immediate supply being brought

to it by the coursing arterial blood. Obviously, the same is true of the oxygen. It takes only a few minutes for the ischemic brain to run out of both before it suffocates. Neurons are extremely sensitive to ischemia; irreversible destructive changes begin within fifteen to thirty minutes of the onset of the deprivation.[4]

Nuland's comments and Joe's experience underscore the bottom line of our discussion. Illness is a struggle with death or, to put it more carefully, illness is a struggle with diminished life, which in its furthest reaches is a struggle with death. Anxiety is the apprehension of this drastic situation.

Even though all illnesses are not so extreme, many illnesses carry the threat of death, if not for medical reasons then certainly because they are perceived that way by the believer who is ill. In any case, pastoral ministry in general, and pastoral preaching in particular, must attend to the individual's struggle. As we have seen, this involves sensitivity to one or more of the five ways in which illness can be experienced. But more important, it means being aware that the individual may be locked into a struggle with life and death, for he or she may stand before the apprehension that life has encountered a malady from which it may never recover.

Preaching to Joe

The first thing to be said about preaching to Joe is that the preacher must proceed carefully. Addressing a particular situation like Joe's from the pulpit may be a violation of confidentiality. And if Joe feels that the sermon is aimed at him, he may be hurt and feel betrayed, especially if he suspects that others in the congregation have also guessed that he is the target of the sermon. In the process, Joe's pastoral relationship with the preacher may be damaged if not destroyed.

Preaching to Joe is best done obliquely rather than directly. There are times for direct communication, for example, when information is being presented or when confrontation is necessary, but generally pastoral preaching thrives on indirection. Fred B. Craddock, in a monograph entitled *Overhearing the Gospel*, makes a strong case for indirect communication. He maintains that when a sermon is not aimed directly at worshipers, a sense of distance is established that actually opens the door to communication. Listeners are given the anonymity and "freedom to reflect and decide out of public view."[5] They feel safe and lower their guard, and consequently they become more engaged. This fact is evident in services like marriage ceremonies and funerals or even in "children's sermons." Participants in these events may begin as eavesdroppers but often become attentive listeners.

Jesus used indirect communication to break through the hardened assumptions of his listeners.

> The parables of Jesus were told to be overheard. "There was a certain man"—anonymous, past tense, somewhere else—nothing here addressed to me. Relax and enjoy the story. And then it happens; I am inside the story, and the door closes behind me.[6]

Actually, much of the Bible is heard by first being overheard. Paul wrote letters to the congregations at Corinth, Philippi, and Rome, and we listen in. The persons we know as Matthew, Mark, Luke, and John addressed their understanding of the gospel to particular congregations in the first century, and we hear the story by overhearing what was said to them. We are not addressed directly, but we are drawn into the story and are addressed by it as we stand at a safe distance.

Preaching from a lectionary contributes to the safety and benefits of indirect communication. The weekly readings are appointed, not chosen. Negatively, this means that the reading for the week may not provide the pastor with an immediate opportunity to address Joe, but positively it means that Joe is unlikely to suspect that the pastor has rummaged through Scripture looking for a text that is imprinted with his name.

Hymns, too, contribute to the indirect communication of the gospel. While they are often addressed to God and are sung to praise God, in the words and music, the congregation hears the good news. "O God, our help in ages past, our hope for years to come, our shelter from the stormy blast, and our eternal home" (*Lutheran Book of Worship*, 320) is a confession of God to God, but in the process we hear words of reassurance.

Finding Out Where Joe Is

As noted earlier, Joe's struggle with emphysema was not a stable state. Instead, as his emphysema progressed, Joe moved from discomfort to pain to panic. The emotions he felt and the questions he asked changed or were intensified. This means that in preparing to preach to Joe, the pastoral preacher must go through a diagnostic process and pinpoint Joe's current condition.

The pastor will be helped in this process if he or she takes a few notes immediately after each pastoral visit or contact. Most "planners," be they electronic or in book form, provide space for notes. Often the look in a person's eyes or the tone of voice or the facial expressions are as critical to the diagnostic process as snatches of dialogue. If the pastor is attentive to these verbal and nonverbal signs, he or she will come away from the visit with a definite sense of how the patient is experiencing his or her illness.

Each pastoral visit, captured in notes, becomes a snapshot of ongoing action. Like photographs, case notes record Joe's situation in terms of a particular time, place, and set of circumstances. The pastoral preacher should not freeze Joe there but should use the snapshot to address him where he is. Eudora Welty, a Pulitzer Prize–winning fiction writer, expresses the point well. "Life doesn't hold still. A good snapshot stopped a moment from running away. Photography taught me that to be able to capture transience, by being ready to click the shutter at the crucial moment, was the greatest need I had."[7]

When it comes time to formulate the sermon, the preacher should try to help listeners face the reality of their suffering. For some listeners, like Joe, that may not be a major task, but in any case, the preacher should help listeners gain a fresh perspective on their illness. Sometimes that is not easy to do, for the last thing parishioners may want to do is to see their illness from a new perspective. In the film *Dead Poets Society,* Robin Williams plays the role of John Keating, a young English teacher at Weldon Academy, somewhere in New England. One day in class, Keating suddenly leaps up on his desk. "Why do I stand here?" he asked. . . . "I stand on my desk to remind myself that we must constantly force ourselves to look at things differently. The world looks different from up here."[8] Keating then challenged each boy to take a turn on the desk. "If you're sure about something," he said as they slowly returned to their seats, "force yourself to think about it another way, even if you know it's wrong or silly. When you read, don't consider only what the author thinks, but take time to consider what you think."[9]

For Joe to take a fresh look at his illness may be enlightening and even freeing. The pastor can encourage this change

- by retelling the story of sickness
- by identifying the emotions being felt and by posing the theological questions being asked
- by focusing on images of sickness that spark the imagination and touch feelings

Sometimes a fresh perspective can be given to the parishioner by using images from literature. Pastors who take time to read fine literature and to see important films are provided with narratives that, when retold in sermons, permit suffering believers like Joe to see their situation in a different light. The narratives are a form of indirect communication in which the person becomes involved in the struggle of others and in the process clarifies his or her own situation.

In John Updike's fourth and final novel about ex-basketball star Harry "Rabbit" Angstrom, Rabbit explores the bleak terrain of late middle age, looking for reasons to live. Like Joe, Rabbit is in his mid-fifties and is ill. He struggles with a brooding anxiety occasioned by serious heart trouble.

> Standing amid the tan, excited post-Christmas crowd at the Southwest Florida Regional Airport, Rabbit Angstrom has a funny sudden feeling that what he has come to meet, what's floating in unseen about to land, is not his son Nelson and daughter-in-law Pru and their two children but something more ominous and intimately his: his own death, shaped vaguely like an airplane. The Sensation chills him, above and beyond the terminal air-conditioning.[10]

Rabbit is overweight, more than 230 pounds at age fifty-five. A former athlete, now out of shape and unable to stick to a diet, he is beset with pains both real and imagined. Like Joe, Rabbit experiences bodily discomfort.

> Sometimes Rabbit's spirit feels as if it might faint from lugging all this body around. Little squeezy pains tease his ribs, reaching into his upper left arm. He has spells of feeling short of breath and mysteriously full in the chest, full of some pressing essence. When he was a kid and had growing pains he would be worried and the

grownups around him laughed them off on his behalf; now he is unmistakably a grownup and must do his own laughing off.[11]

Rabbit's painful awareness of his own mortality causes him to be obsessed with death. "A sense of doom regrows its claws around his heart: little prongs like those that hold fast a diamond solitaire."[12] He recalls the accidental drowning of his infant daughter Rebecca thirty years before. He thinks about the explosion that brought down the Pan Am 747 over Scotland. He sees "bodies with hearts pumping tumbling down in the dark . . . like wet melon seeds."[13]

The preacher finds evocative images of anxiety and death in Updike's narrative. But the preacher must be careful. Certain images may be effective in a novel when the reader is curled up in an easy chair, but they may be ineffective, or even offensive, in public proclamation. Joe may not be helped by the image of "bodies tumbling down like wet melon seeds," while he may find that other images, like human life being described as "dust in an air duct," are helpful expressions of his own anxiety about the transitoriness of life.

Part of the diagnostic process is to assess the theological or spiritual struggle of the person who is ill. Rabbit's quarrel with God, for example, is different than Joe's. Joe felt condemned by God. Rabbit also struggled with a sense of guilt, but he questioned God's inaction and God's valuing of human life. Regarding his daughter's drowning, Rabbit ponders: "God hadn't pulled the plug [to let the water out of the tub]. It would have been so easy for Him, Who set the stars in place."[14] The pastoral preacher, knowing the particular theological struggle of Joe and of Rabbit, would address each of them in a different way. For Joe the assurance of God's forgiveness may be primary; for Rabbit the image of God as suffering with those who grieve may be primary.

While great literature can supply us with evocative images, we must also say that its offerings are not always usable in sermons, or at least they are seldom useable exactly as they are written. Nevertheless, pastoral preachers will discover that fine literature, theatrical plays, and dramatic films are significant occasions of overhearing. All of them present an illuminating look into the recesses of the human condition, and therefore they can help the pastoral preacher to address suffering believers. Worshipers hear the voice of their own illness by overhearing the cry of others.

Addressing Joe's Anxiety

Several years ago one of the authors went through an extended period of intense anxiety, primarily at night during the process of falling asleep. It was a time of significant loss for the author. Recently, he had given up a teaching career that had extended over twenty-seven years. He had moved from familiar surroundings into a different house in a different city. He lost the security of his home congregation and had to find another church.

The anxiety was unrelenting. It disturbed the author's sleep at night and cast a shadow of doubt and fear on his daylight hours. The anxiety persisted in spite of many attempts to get it under control. The author was near the end of the proverbial rope, since the panic attacks were earth shaking and no end seemed to be in sight.

When the author finally went to a psychotherapist, they spent the first session reviewing recent events and clarifying the circumstances of the attacks. At the end of the session, the therapist suggested certain "home remedies" and then said softly but with confidence, "We will gain control over the anxiety." Suddenly a great weight was lifted from the author's shoulders. The anxiety had not been wiped away, but someone who stood alongside him had said that it was not interminable.

Further research into the panic attacks traced them back to a sleep disorder, and when the author was put on a CPAP (Continuous Positive Airway Pressure) machine the attacks disappeared. The author was greatly relieved, to say the least, but to this day the therapist's assurance that there was hope in the midst of chaos was a moment of great encouragement.

Pastoral preaching alone may not be able to address the author's anxiety. Neither can it serve as a sole solution for Joe's anxiety. But along with the care of the physician and the care of the pastor, the pastoral preacher is on the front line. He or she must bring the resources of the church to bear on the assaults of serious or life-threatening illness.

Paul Tillich maintains that courage—"the courage to be"[15]—is the antidote to anxiety. The English word *courage* is derived from the Latin term for heart. The Romans had a biological view of the heart and thought that it was the center of human functioning. Thus they spoke about "taking heart" or "being strong of heart."

They were not referring to situations of momentary discomfort but to situations of severe danger or challenge.

Courage does not eradicate anxiety, but it holds it at tolerable limits, just as it did when the therapist's words encouraged one of us. Viktor Frankl, a Jewish psychotherapist who survived Hitler's Auschwitz, writes about the relation of courage and despair from personal experience.

> The death rate in the week between Christmas 1944 and New Year's 1945 increased in camp beyond all previous experience. . . . The explanation for this increase did not lie in the harder working conditions or the deterioration of our food supplies or the change of weather or new epidemics. It was simply that the majority of the prisoners had lived in the naive hope that they would be home again by Christmas. As the time drew near and there was no encouraging news, the prisoners lost courage and disappointment overcame them.[16]

Courage and faith are also closely linked. Both are rooted in God's power and steadfastness, and each reinforces the other: Faith in God gives us courage, while courage strengthens our faith when it becomes feeble or laced with doubt. We remember the promises God made to the people of old. We are assured that God does not forsake us.

> In all his promises the Lord keeps faith,
> he is unchanging in all his works;
> the Lord holds up those who stumble
> and straightens backs which are bent.
> (Ps. 145:13-14 NEB)

Other passages that testify to God's presence among us in sickness and adversity include:

- Psalm 121: Help comes from the Lord.
- Isa. 35:1-10: God promises the Lord's coming.
- Isa. 61:1-3: Good tidings are given to the afflicted.
- Rom. 8:18-23: We await the redemption of our bodies.
- Rom. 8:31-39: Nothing can separate us from the love of God.
- 2 Cor. 1:3-5: God comforts us in affliction.

In the life, death, and resurrection of Jesus Christ, God uniquely demonstrates a firm commitment to persons in distress. Because we believe that God the Father gave the Son to suffer for us, we come to trust that God both understands our suffering and identifies with us as suffering believers. With Dietrich Bonhoeffer, our sighs indicate that "only a suffering God can help."

The lectionary offers opportunities to preach about courage in the face of anxiety. All Saints Sunday, with appointed texts like Isa. 26:1-4, urges us to put our "trust in the Lord forever, for in the Lord God you have an everlasting rock." On this and other special days the preacher can focus on the God-given courage and faith of saints and witnesses, past and present. The Eleventh Sunday after Pentecost uses a text from Hebrews to cite many examples of faithful leaders who exhibited courage and faith and from whose example suffering believers can take heart.

> Time would fail me to tell of Gideon, Barak, Samson, Jephthah, of David and Samuel and the prophets—who through faith conquered kingdoms, administered justice, obtained promises, shut the mouths of lions, quenched raging fire, escaped the edge of the sword, won strength out of weakness. (Heb. 11:32–34)

The writer concludes his "profiles in courage" with an exhortation to look to Jesus, the true source of both courage and faith.

> Therefore, since we are surrounded by so great a cloud of witnesses, let us also lay aside every weight and the sin that clings so closely, and let us run with perseverance the race that is set before us, looking to Jesus the pioneer and perfecter of our faith, who for the sake of the joy that was set before him endured the cross, disregarding its shame, and has taken his seat at the right hand of the throne of God. (Heb. 12:1-2)

Pastoral preaching can use any one of these resources to speak to Joe. The witness of the saints may help him to bear his illness with courage. The outcome is not guaranteed, but God's promise in Scripture combined with the empathic message of the pastoral preacher can lend a measure of courage to Joe's discouraged spirit. The pastoral preacher must be diligent in planting the seed but trustful in leaving the growth of the seed up to God.

Preaching to Sickness Generally

As pastoral preachers face the general task of preaching to those who are ill, they have a plethora of biblical resources available to them. As Morton T. Kelsey observes, "Nearly one-fifth of the entire Gospels is devoted to Jesus' healing and the discussions occasioned by it. . . . Forty-one distinct instances of physical and mental healing are recorded in the four Gospels (there are seventy-two accounts in all, including duplications). . . ."[17] In Mark's account alone there are six references to healings in a scant thirty-six verses (1:21—2:12).[18]

The New Testament references to healing are often rich with christological claim. The third evangelist narrates how the imprisoned John the Baptist, uncertain if Jesus was the Messiah, sent messengers to him asking, "Are you the one who is to come, or are we to wait for another?" Jesus answers the question by pointing to what his ministry has done for those with physical afflictions: "Go and tell John what you have seen and heard: the blind receive their sight, the lame walk, the lepers are cleansed, the deaf hear, the dead are raised, the poor have good news brought to them" (Luke 7:18-23). In another context, Jesus interprets his exorcisms, his casting out of demons, as a sign of the power of God on behalf of the people: "If it is by the finger of God that I cast out the demons, then the kingdom of God has come to you" (Luke 11:20).

Healing stories are featured prominently in lectionaries. The Fourth Gospel's story of the healing of a man born blind (John 9:1-41) is one example. If there are no particular instances of blindness in the congregation, a narrative like John 9 may not speak directly to the assembled members. At such times, the exercise "What's it like to be. . . ?" may enlist the congregation's attention and may give concrete detail and a realistic tone to the sermon.[19] The reality and hardship of being blind became more real to a group of lay leaders as they considered "What's it like

- to never see a sunset?
- to stumble over unseen obstacles?
- to need help to travel here and there?
- to be disabled?
- to feel dependent and sometimes foolish?

- to sense people staring?
- to be different?

The pastoral preacher who selects John 9 should remember that for the evangelist the healing of the blind man is a sign that Christ is the light in a dark world. And the mode of healing, washing in the Pool of Siloam, strongly suggests a connection to baptism, known in the early church as "illumination" *(photismos)*.[20] A critical dimension of the story is the gradual deepening of the blind man's spiritual sight (faith). At first, when he is questioned by his neighbors about the healing, he says that the healing was done by "the man called Jesus." When he is interrogated by the Pharisees, he testifies of Jesus, "He is a prophet." When he is called before the religious authorities a second time, he avers, "If this man were not from God, he could do nothing." Later in the day when Jesus and the blind man meet, the blind man worships Jesus as Son of Man (John 9:11-38). For the former beggar, physical sight has become faith sight.

The story reminds us that God may become known to us as we struggle with the negative experiences of daily life. As we try to make sense of sickness and other sufferings, God's care and love may be revealed to us. Of course, this outcome is far from certain, for the Pharisees become progressively blind as Jesus works in their very midst. Nevertheless, our incarnational theology affirms that God is revealed behind, around, and through the experiences that comprise our lives. And what about the person who prays for healing of mind, body, or spirit without any apparent relief? Liturgies for healing provide theological themes, suggestive images, and helpful prayers for the preacher's reflection and use. For example, along with continued prayer for recovery, sufferers can pray for strength to bear suffering and for the peace of God.

> Merciful Lord, you sent your Son to be our peace. Help all who suffer pain or grief to find in him strength and peace, so that their trust in your promises may be renewed, through Jesus Christ our Lord.[21]

This prayer urges us to live in hope, not in the shallow reassurance that if we believe in God our pain will disappear but in the hope that is summed up in the word *God*. Christian hope is confidence in

God. It is the assurance that God keeps promises. It is "trust in God when everything seems hopeless." And this trust in God is active, even aggressive, which is to say that illness is not to be endured stoically by Christians. Resignation in the face of loss is not a biblical option. While the Bible is bluntly honest about the reality of suffering, it does not condone passive despair. Paul is upbeat as he speaks of discipleship as suffering with Christ.

> We boast in our hope of sharing the glory of God. And not only that, but we also boast in our sufferings, knowing that suffering produces endurance, and endurance produces character, and character produces hope, and hope does not disappoint us, because God's love has been poured into our hearts through the Holy Spirit that has been given to us. (Rom. 5:2-5)

For believers, then, suffering and pain "involve processes that we do not simply go through but that we grow through."[22] In a determined reliance on a living God rather than on human strength, faith is renewed. When the struggle is engaged actively, believers find fresh hope and renewed life.

Conclusion

In seeking to address suffering individuals from the pulpit, pastoral preaching is best done obliquely rather than directly. Indirect communication may use concrete human experiences from the world of literature, film, and theatre as well as from biblical narratives to evoke listener insight.

Through the preached word, persons like Joe can find an antiphon to their anxiety. They are imbued with a courage that they did not know they had as the preacher utilizes some of the numerous instances of God-given courage that are found in Scripture or in the lives of suffering believers, past or present.

New Testament accounts of Jesus' own healings underscore the power of God over the forces of evil at the same time they testify to the inauguration of the promised kingdom in a world still being saved. Hope is alive in a community that can help sufferers experience joy in Christ in the midst of negation. The Nikolai Grundvig hymn "O Day Full of Grace" pulsates with such hope and joy.

When we on that final journey go
That Christ is for us preparing,
We'll gather in song, our hearts aglow,
All joy of the heavens sharing,
And walk in the light of God's own place,
With angels his name adoring.

(*Lutheran Book of Worship*, 161)

7

Preaching to Believers
Who Experience Violence

VIOLENCE IS AS WIDE AS LIFE AND AS POWERFUL AS DEATH. It can be experienced in physical and emotional, in verbal and nonverbal, in familial and social ways. It can be a prolonged "put down" that eats away at one's integrity or a sudden and deadly blow that extinguishes one's life in a fateful moment.

Generally, pastoral preachers seem to find it easier to address violence that occurs on a social level, but they must also be concerned about violence that occurs on a personal level, especially if that violence occurs in the home. To make our discussion more personal, we will focus not just on the experience of violence but on a particular person who has been violated. Rollo May, in his *Power and Innocence: A Search for the Sources of Violence*, offers a case study of a thirty-two-year-old woman whom he calls Mercedes.[1]

Mercedes was referred to May by her husband's therapist. She had been seen by two other therapists before May. Both of them had concluded that she could not be helped by therapy because she lacked the motivation for intense therapy and because she was not introspective enough to go through the arduous analytical process. May did not believe it but instead felt that the real challenge was to find a modality of therapy that would be appropriate to this particular patient.

Mercedes had been married for eight years, but the marriage was in danger of collapsing, "partly because of Mercedes' so-called frigidity and complete lack of sexual interest in her husband."[2] In spite of her indifference to sex, Mercedes' dominant desire was to have a baby. She had gotten pregnant several times, but each time she either had a miscarriage or she had to have an abortion for one reason or another. She came to May feeling that nothing could be done to resolve her predicament.

Early in therapy, May learned that Mercedes was a long-time victim of violence. Since the age of eleven to the time she turned twenty-one, her stepfather "had used her as a prostitute." Several times a week he would arrange for her to have sex with men of his choosing. If he received money for these "visits," Mercedes never saw a penny of it. The subservience to the stepfather's wishes, let alone the meeting of the demands that the clients put on her, continued throughout Mercedes' years in college. "It was only when she went to nursing school after college and lived out of her mother's house that she broke away from her stepfather."[3]

On the one hand, Mercedes was docile and submissive. Without raising any question, she tried to please her stepfather and, more generally, she seemed passively "to accept whatever form of victimization life might bring her." On the other hand, she could stand up for herself and, if necessary, become physically combative. "She had fought not only her own battles at school and on the street—in which she would go into a wild fury—but had also protected her younger brother as he grew up."[4] In regard to the prostitution, she seemed devoid of feeling for a long time. When she finally showed some emotion about it, it took the form of a childhood memory. She recalled a visit to relatives in Virginia and described a scene where a donkey was trying to copulate with a "mare which stood there apathetically." She ended the story with a vehement "I hated that donkey!" May saw in the remembrance how much she "regarded the prostitution as a hated offense against" herself.[5]

Mercedes was, in many ways, an empty vessel. She did not have many wishes of her own. She also did not have many feelings of her own. When asked what she wanted to get out of therapy, she thought for a long time and then said that she often found herself praying "a kind of prayer: 'Let me have a child, let me be a good wife, let me enjoy sex, let me *feel* something.'"[6] The urge to be something, even if it was only the urge to be something that might please others, was there, but it was buried deeply under the acts of violence that had been perpetrated against her.

The Pastoral Significance of Violence

In Mercedes' case, being violated involves at least five interrelated experiences, and each one has a decidedly deleterious effect on her development.

Being Desecrated

The self can be defined in various ways, for example, as the totality of the person or as that portion of the total person that is owned or recognized as "me" or "I." However defined, the self is constituted by certain boundaries and should enjoy certain inalienable rights. Paul Tillich, for example, says that "it belongs to the right of everyone whom we encounter to demand something from us, at least that even in the most impersonal relations the other one is acknowledged as a person."[7]

Mercedes did not receive anything like due consideration. Her boundaries were transgressed by the evil arrangements of a lustful stepfather, and she was invaded in the most private spheres of her life by the men who had sex with her. She was desecrated not once but innumerable times.

What Mercedes experienced goes against what Martin Buber calls the "human order of things" or, to put it more personally, she was reduced to an impersonal object whose very being was forced to serve the sensual desires of other people. To preserve some semblance of integrity, Mercedes shut down and became what she had to become in order to survive—a vacuous nonfeeling vessel with no rights of her own. In the midst of this morass, Mercedes no doubt retained a fragment of integrity, however small, but anything like the full stature of who she was and of what she could become was lost to the violent invasion of her innermost self.

Being desecrated works its evil consequences. It shatters the self and makes any solid and worthwhile identity impossible. The self is profaned, which psychologically is a very real kind of death. Mercedes became aware of this consequence through an experience she called "death in the dentist's chair." She agreed to her dentist's urging to go through an unpleasant dental procedure by taking gas. Once under the gas, Mercedes experienced the doom of death. She was convinced that she was going to die. She cried silently through the whole procedure but did not have the strength to tell the dentist to stop the gas. The feeling of sadness and the struggle with depression lingered long after the procedure. She was still crying uncontrollably when she saw May two days later.

Through her encounter with death, Mercedes became aware of the "preciousness of life," but even more important she became convinced "that she had as much right to live as any other human being."[8] This assurance was a streak of light across a darkened sky. She had lived a life of denial and self-abnegation, believing that given what had happened to her she did not deserve to enjoy life, let alone to affirm herself. By being desecrated she felt that she had forfeited her right to be the person she was. Only after many hours of therapy and the paradigmatic experience of dying in the dentist's chair was she able to assert her right to live.

Being Exposed

If being desecrated cheapens the self, it also exposes the self, if not to the world, then certainly to the self and to the people who violate the self. The self's boundaries and defenses are torn down, and the self stands naked before the eyes that behold it.

To be exposed is to experience shame. The self is defenseless against its own involuntary disclosure, and it is vulnerable to the degradation of its own exposed and unacceptable image. W. Somerset Maugham, in his novel *Of Human Bondage,* gives us a telling example of shame.[9] Philip, a lonely and sensitive youth with a club foot, was going through an extended search to find himself. He was sent to a boarding school and assigned to a room with several other boys. That evening Philip was in his cubicle when a couple of roommates came in and demanded that Philip show them his club foot. Philip refused. One of the boys grabbed his arm and began to twist it. Philip, withstanding the torment, gave "a sob and a gasp" but still refused. The bully applied more pressure. The pain became intolerable. Philip caved in and stuck his foot out from under the blanket. The boys gazed at the foot and called it "beastly." Philip was humiliated and shamed. He put his teeth into the pillow so his sobbing would not be audible. Maugham explains: "[Philip] was not crying for the pain they had caused him, nor for the humiliation he had suffered when they looked at his foot, but with rage at himself because, unable to stand the torture, he had put out his foot of his own accord."[10]

Never mind that Philip made a decision while suffering excruciating pain. He still failed to measure up to the expectation that he should not have given in to the boys' demands. Consequently, the humiliation he suffered when they looked at and made fun of his club foot gave way to the deeper shame that he was weak and had failed. He was a traitor to his own resolve, and that unfaithfulness caused a severe sense of shame.

Unlike Philip, May's description of Mercedes' story does not bring out the dynamic of exposure and shame, but that does not mean that it was not there. Surely there was shame for Mercedes in being prostituted, but the deeper shame may have been what she did to herself. She prostituted herself, sacrificing her own internal standards or expectations, in the name of trying to please someone else. The incongruity between herself and her behavior was exposed, explicitly or implicitly, in every act of violence against her.

Being Rendered Powerless

Violence is about power, about taking power away from the victim and about assuming power on the part of the perpetrator. May talks about five levels of power. At the most basic and primitive level is the power to be, the power to exist as a living creature and the primordial desire to receive the necessary sustenance to remain alive. The power to be does not remain a general drive. It becomes personal and takes the form of affirming oneself as a living creature. This second level of power, the power of self-affirmation, is the self acknowledging itself as a being of significance and worth. This level of power is not so much an achievement of the self as it is a product of being treated as significant by those who are significant to us. If self-affirmation is denied, the power to be is elevated to the level of self-assertion. The individual pushes his or her right to be recognized as a person, specifically as a person of value and influence. The fourth level of power, aggression, kicks in when "self-assertion is blocked over a period of time." The individual asserts himself or herself by assuming positions of power, even by moving into "the territory of another and by taking possession of some of it for one's self."[11] If all else fails, the individual moves from aggression to violence. The individual lashes out, often physically though sometimes psychologically, and seeks to bring about his or her just due by force.

Mercedes' complete capitulation to her stepfather's wishes appears to be a symptom of her sense of powerlessness. Her reaction to May's attempt to draw out her anger was even more telling. Her dreams, as interpreted by May, indicated that the "mother, and less frequently her father or others, were attacking and trying to kill her." But May could not get her to acknowledge how she "must feel toward her assassins. . . . It became clear that she was totally unable to muster any conscious rage toward her mother or stepfather or toward others who were out to kill her."[12]

On May's scale of power, Mercedes lived on a primitive level. She had the urge to exist as a living creature (the power to be), though sometimes that was even in jeopardy, but a life of violation had stripped her of any power to affirm or to assert herself. On rare occasions when she asserted power, she did so mostly on her brother's behalf and then only by going into "a wild fury" (violence). Not even going to college and having the support of her sorority empowered her to stand up for herself. It was only after she got out of her mother's house that she began to move beyond the crippling effects of powerlessness.

Being Made Guilty

In a way, we have already touched on this point. We saw that being violated induces shame, the shame of having some portion of one's unacceptable self exposed. Ironically, the individual may also experience and take on the shame of the violator. For example, Mercedes may not only experience her own shame. She may also experience the shame of the men who visited her, if not by being associated with them ("birds of a feather flock together"), then by taking some responsibility, however irrational, for their shameful acts. It is as though she tempted them to do what they did.

Shame must be distinguished from guilt. As we have seen, shame deals with a sense of inadequacy, with a failure to measure up to one's expectations. Guilt, in distinction, has to do with trans-gres-sion, with crossing over a line or with disobeying a rule that should be honored. Guilt is a loss of innocence and comes with a threat of punishment. These two faces of guilt, the loss of innocence and the fear of punishment, contribute to the entangled nature of violence.

Mercedes did not cross over the line of her own accord. She was pushed or, given her tender age, we might even say her stepfather forced her. In this sense she is not guilty. But that is not the end of the story. Mercedes has to contend with her own conscience, with what she feels she should have done but failed to do. We can assume that at some point her conscience told her not to go along with her stepfather's plans, told her to be strong enough to say no. Nevertheless, she did not resist. In this sense she becomes guilty in her own eyes even if not in the eyes of others.

Becoming guilty carries with it the threat of punishment. Not only may Mercedes feel that she deserves to be punished but also she may in various ways punish herself for what she has done. Her whole life of self-abnegation may be a form of self-punishment. And her inability to carry and give birth to a child may be a concrete way of paying back the debt of guilt.

Our analysis of Mercedes' situation may not be exhaustive of her struggle, but it serves to illustrate how insidious a sense of guilt can be. We can hold ourselves responsible for what we do, even though there are major forces in violence that push us in a certain direction and that keep us going along the same path. While being violated may seriously impair our ability to reason or to resist, it does not relieve us of all responsibility. We may still hold ourselves accountable for what we have done or what we have failed to do.

Being Angry

Mercedes lived with anger or even rage, though she was the last one to know it or to admit it. May hypothesized that it was there, but he had no evidence of it until Mercedes began to bleed vaginally and then in therapy began to report a dream. As indicated in an earlier discussion, the dreams usually involved aggression toward Mercedes with her mother and, less frequently, her father attempting to kill her. May became intrigued by the close relationship between the dreams and the bleeding. Because the bleeding was seen as "a harbinger of a miscarriage,"[13] May felt that something had to be done to express Mercedes' locked-up anger. Since Mercedes could not do that, May himself began to step into her place and vent the anger. "Each time she began vaginal bleeding and brought in . . . a dream, I would verbally counterattack those who were trying to kill her. Chiefly I attacked her mother with other figures thrown in from time to time."[14]

Mercedes remained silent during May's tirade, but shortly the bleeding would stop. Each time there was the danger of a miscarriage, therefore, May would launch into an attack, "expressing the aggression [that Mercedes] could not, or did not dare to, feel." After several months, Mercedes "began to feel her own aggression and expressed her own anger at the attackers in the dream."[15] She even called up her parents separately and told them that they were not to contact her until after the birth. The venting of anger worked its miracle. Mercedes gave birth to a healthy male child; and in recognition of this blessing, she gave him a name like Prometheus that signified "a new beginning in the history of mankind."[16]

Anger can be a healthy and legitimate reaction to violence. May's five levels of power indicate that anger, and even violence, is a natural response to those who would destroy our power to be or our right to be recognized as a person of value and worth. Yet anger, even justified anger, is often seen as unacceptable, something that should not be acknowledged, let alone expressed. This seems especially true of those whose self-esteem has been decimated by violence and invasion.

Preaching to Mercedes

Rollo May's therapeutic attempt to speak for Mercedes when she could not speak for herself offers us a clue about preaching to those who have suffered violence. Violence is often so destructive of one's being that those who are violated need someone to give voice to their pain and devastation. They need someone to speak for them, but the one who speaks must speak in a way that empowers the violated person eventually to speak for himself or herself. That is the baseline of our pastoral preaching as we seek to address Mercedes.

What was stated in chapter 6 regarding preaching to Joe is worth repeating here. The preacher must be scrupulous not to violate confidence. If Mercedes even guesses that a sermon is directed at her, she will experience further violation and shame. Instead of being empowered to speak for herself, her ability to communicate may be compromised further.

Preaching to Mercedes, like preaching to Joe, is best done obliquely. Indirect communication will actually open the door to communication. While direct address raises defenses, indirect address should cause Mercedes to lower her guard and should help her to overhear the gospel.

The Bondage of Vicious Circles

In order to speak for Mercedes, it is critical for communicators to understand how difficult it is to be helpful to persons who are caught in a whirlpool of desecration, exposure, powerlessness, guilt, and anger. They often find themselves in a vicious circle, that is, in a situation in which any attempt to solve a given problem results in the aggravation of the problem or the creation of a worse one. Situations of poverty, pollution, and violence often breed vicious circles. Persons, such as prisoners, migrant workers, or mentally ill people, are often caught in uncontrollable swirls and are drawn steadily downward.[17] Even the best human effort to break the chains of bondage can prove to be impotent and can lead to greater enslavement.

There is an important structural analogy between the apostle Paul's bondages of law, sin, and death (Rom. 7:7-11) and the vicious circle of violence. As humans cannot extract themselves from Paul's "enemies," so too they may find themselves drawn underwater in the currents of violence. The attempt to break free of sin may create a legalistic allegiance to the law; the attempt to break free of violence may bring further desecration and destruction upon oneself. If Mercedes had tried to stop the stepfather's "arrangements" by enlisting the help of her mother, she may have suffered further humiliation and been confirmed in her feeling that she was an evil and unworthy person.

Liberation from sin and its attendant guilt is not a human possibility. It is the free gift of God to those who believe. And this emancipation may bring some psychological release with it. A reconstituted relationship with God may make it possible for Mercedes to experience herself as a cherished child of God, and therefore she may begin to see herself as a creature worthy of more than the stepfather's violations.

Pastoral preaching rests on the possibility (hope) that redemption theologically can open violated humans to holistic healing and transformation. In the autobiography of his own grief, C. S. Lewis testifies both to the reality of a spiral from which he could not break free and to the release that God was able to give.

And so, perhaps, with God. I have gradually been coming to feel that the door is no longer shut and bolted. Was it my own frantic need that slammed it in my face? The time when there is nothing at all in your soul except a cry for help may be just the time when God can't give it: you are like the drowning man who can't be helped because he clutches and grabs. Perhaps your own reiterated cries deafen you to the voice you hoped to hear.[18]

In the process of release, both the cross and the resurrection of Christ are key symbols. As faith experiences the crucified one, the believer is able to accept an existence impregnated with pain and violence. He or she sees that Jesus also was betrayed, was exposed to public humiliation, and was hung on a cross. As faith experiences the resurrected one, the believer is able to live into the future with hope. He or she is able to understand that in the midst of violation and powerlessness, Christ brings the promise of new life.

Speaking for Mercedes

As pastoral preaching gives voice to the pain of violated persons like Mercedes, it empowers them to begin to acknowledge their pain. As we noted earlier, suffering often reduces afflicted people to silence. Our rose-colored culture does not support the language of deep pain. Thus Mercedes is left alone with her own inarticulated sighs.

The pastoral preacher does not serve Mercedes well by giving vent to her pain by emotional outbursts. A coherent and common "language of lament" must be found.[19] The book of Psalms has long provided such a language for worshipers. Clergy will find in the lectionaries particular psalms that express or amplify the believer's suffering. Psalm 22, appointed for Good Friday, provides graphic language for violated people to articulate pain, including the pain of feeling forsaken by God and others.[20]

> My God, my God, why have you forsaken me?
> Why are you so far from helping me, from the words of my
>   groaning? . . .
> But I am a worm and not human;
>   scorned by others and despised by the people.
> All who see me mock at me; they make mouths at me,
> they . . . shake their heads. (Ps. 22:1, 6-7)

The psalms that are particularly helpful for preaching are those that include the reality of suffering and the hope of God's assistance. For example, in the season of Lent, Year C of the *Revised Common Lectionary*, the following psalms provide a helpful language. Psalm 51 expresses a desire for cleansing from sin: "Create in me a clean heart, O God, and put a new and right spirit within me" (Ps. 51:10). Psalm 27 asks for God's help in the day of trouble and in the face of adversaries: "False witnesses have risen against me, and they are breathing out violence" (v. 12). The theme of guilt and forgiveness is plain in Psalm 32: "I said, 'I will confess my transgressions to the LORD,' and you forgave the guilt of my sin" (v. 5). Psalm 126 prays, "May those who sow in tears reap with shouts of joy" (v. 5).

In speaking to Mercedes, the preacher may choose a psalm that is read or intoned in worship. If so, the psalmist's own cries of pain and distress, expressed forcefully, can be elaborated by the addition of biblical and contemporary expressions of pain.

> With the writer of Psalm 22, many of us shout,
> Why does this abuse continue?
> Why are we shamed in front of neighbors and friends?
> Why are we mocked?
> Are you mute, God?
> Have you fallen asleep?
> When will this cup of suffering pass?
>
> We cry as Jesus did from the cross:
> "My God, my God, why have you forsaken me?
> Why are you so far from helping me, from the words of my groaning?"

Good News for Mercedes

The Gospel of Luke tells of Jesus' hospitality to persons who are estranged by the religious and social mores of their day. In Luke 7:36—8:3, the pastoral preacher will find the story of a woman who crashed a social gathering in Jesus' honor at the house of Simon the Pharisee.[21] As Mercedes, or others in the congregation whose boundaries have been transgressed, are drawn into the narrative and the sermon, they may be able to overhear the gospel and be affirmed as persons of significance and worth in God's eyes.

Though we are not told the details of the woman's sin, it appears to be public knowledge. Whether she was a prostitute or not (Luke omits the word), she apparently was a person who subjected herself to misuse and abuse. Simon's table fellowship does not extend to women as a group, and certainly it does not extend to this woman. Her appearance evoked disgust from Simon and most likely disapproval from his guests.

When the woman approached Jesus with her alabaster jar of ointment and began to anoint his feet as he reclined at table, disgust turned to judgment. The woman wept openly and used her tears to bathe Jesus' feet. She knelt, kissed his feet, and dried them with her hair. Simon fumed inwardly: "If this man were a prophet, he would have known who and what kind of woman this is who is touching him—that she is a sinner" (Luke 7:39).

Jesus knew. Instead of censuring her and pushing her deeper into the deadly whirlpool, he rebuked Simon. "You gave me no water for my feet . . . no kiss . . . no ointment." It was true. Simon had not extended to Jesus the courtesies of hospitality that had been given by the woman. Then Jesus turned to the woman and said, "Your sins are forgiven. . . . Your faith has saved you; go in peace" (Luke 7:48, 50). We can assume from the text that Simon's lesser debt is also canceled (Luke 7:41-43), so both the judging Pharisee and the violated woman hear good news of forgiveness.

In many churches this good news is enacted liturgically. For example, in the "Brief Order for Confession and Forgiveness" in the *Lutheran Book of Worship,* worshipers regularly affirm both the reality of sin as individual acts of disobedience and the reality of sin as a vicious circle that imprisons

> Most merciful God, we confess that we are in bondage to sin and cannot free ourselves. We have sinned against you in thought, word, and deed, by what we have done and by what we have left undone.[22]

The preacher should take the opportunity to interpret the theological significance of this act of confession. Worshipers are opening themselves up to the good news that Jesus Christ was given by God to die and to rise again for believers who, like Mercedes, are unable to free themselves from the vortex (downdraft) of sin. This liberation can lead to a life in Christ that is open to the transforming work of God's Spirit. This possibility is announced by the worship leader in the words, "To those who believe in Jesus Christ [God] gives the power to become the children of God and bestows on them the Holy Spirit."[23]

The pastoral preacher may also want to note that Jesus' encounter with the woman who was a sinner occurs at table. This scene has eucharistic significance. Liturgically speaking, the Eucharist, which is a feast of suffering and victorious love, acts out the good news of forgiveness and reconciliation. Paul's words, incorporated in most liturgies of Holy Communion, are to the point: "For as often as you eat this bread and drink the cup, you proclaim the Lord's death until he comes" (1 Cor. 11:26). The sacrament looks back to Jesus' own sufferings on Calvary. At the same time, the meal is filled with eschatological promise. Participation in the meal affirms that God's action in the past is living and efficacious in the present. And the act of eating and drinking proclaims that the risen Christ is present and that participants are included in the new life of the Holy Spirit until Jesus comes again.

Preaching to Violence Generally

We have said that violence is often so destructive of one's being that those who are violated need someone to give voice to their pain and devastation. They need someone to speak for them in a way that empowers them to speak for themselves.

One of the authors experienced this need when he was mugged. Prior to the mugging, his home had been burglarized, and electronic equipment along with irreplaceable family heirlooms, like class rings, gold watches, and jewelry had been taken. The family felt violated but found it easy to express their anger. It was different, however, when the author was robbed at gunpoint on a Philadelphia street. He found it much more difficult to verbalize the trauma. In fact, friends had to help him identify and articulate feelings of rage and betrayal. Only when they first spoke for him could he acknowledge and express his deep-seated feelings.

In preaching about violence to congregants, a series of brief vignettes may help to draw a variety of persons into the sermonic event. In older rhetorical manuals, this kind of series was sometimes

called a "string of pearls." In his sermon "Praying through Clenched
Teeth," Fred B. Craddock creates such a string.

> I am going to say a word, and the moment I say the word I want
> you to see a face, to recall a face and a name, someone who comes
> to mind when I say the word. Are you ready? The word is "bitter."
> Bitter. Do you see a face? I see a face. I see the face of a farmer in
> western Oklahoma riding a mortgaged tractor, burning gasoline
> purchased on credit, moving across rented land, rearranging the
> dust. Bitter.
>
> Do you see a face? I see the face of a woman forty-seven years
> old. She sits out on a hillside, drawn and confused under a green
> canopy furnished by the mortuary. She is banked on all sides by
> flowers sprinkled with cards: "You have our condolences." Bitter.
>
> Do you see a face? I see the face of a man who runs a small gro-
> cery store. His father ran the store in that neighborhood for
> twenty years, and he is now in his twelfth year there. The grocery
> doesn't make much profit, but it keeps the family together. It's a
> business. There are no customers in the store now, and the grocer
> stands in the doorway with his apron rolled up around his waist,
> looking across the street where workmen are completing a super-
> market. Bitter.[24]

Craddock adds a few more "pearls" to the string before he turns
to the story of Saul of Tarsus, whose bitterness caused him to pursue the followers of Jesus to have them arrested and put to death.
Craddock's pearls, or others like them, could be used to form a helpful string on the theme of violence. But the preacher needs to
remember that the chief authority for believers is Scripture. Contemporary images and stories like Craddock's have their place in
pastoral preaching, but issues like violence need to have a biblical
anchor, much like Craddock gave for bitterness by pointing to Saul
of Tarsus.

Jesus often used parables to dramatize his point and to make
contact with his listeners. One of his parables, Luke's "the good
Samaritan," is a story of violence. It can be used to make different
points, depending on which character in the story is highlighted. As
listeners hear the narrative, most of them will be drawn to the helpful Samaritan, the "good guy." With this focus, the parable becomes
an example story, a comparison of the selfish concern of the priest
and Levite with the unselfish love of the hated Samaritan. Listeners

are encouraged to act as the Samaritan did, to assist victims of violence to promote healing.

The focus of the story could be put on the man in the ditch. If this is done, the meaning and the intention of the parable changes. The man, who surely expected help from persons of his own faith and race, was left beaten and half dead. From an unexpected source, from a half-breed heretic, he received abundant help, more than he could ever imagine. If, as some commentators believe, the original parable ended with the question "Which of these three, do you think, was a neighbor to the man who fell into the hands of the robbers?" (Luke 10:36) the narrative becomes a challenge to its listeners. If told by a rabbi to a Jewish audience, the story challenges the listener's worldview, since clerics become bad and Samaritans become good. If preached today, listeners are challenged to see themselves both as allies who do not help the needy and as victims who are sometimes saved by strangers, even by undesirable strangers.

In the early days of the HIV/AIDS epidemic, a Philadelphia newspaper reported that members of the nursing staff in a local hospital refused to care for a dying patient. The patient was a white homosexual person in an advanced stage of the disease. Hattie, a Baptist Christian and an African American woman with small children at home, volunteered to work double shifts until help could be found. "He's one of God's children," she said as she gave concrete expression to God's mercy.

Hattie posits an implicit link between healing and proclamation. Jesus made the link explicit when he sent out the Seventy. He instructed the seventy to enter villages and to "cure the sick who are there, and say to them, 'The kingdom of God has come near to you'" (Luke 10:9).

In our ministry, the link between healing and God's good news is often far less evident. This is especially true in cases of violence. God's healing power is seldom an extraordinary act of effecting an immediate cure or of eliminating deep pain by a simple touch or an instant word. Less miraculous means also represent the empowerment of the Spirit. If pastoral preachers can communicate genuine care to those who have been violated or if they can empower the violated to go for professional help or if they can live out the good news of God's unconditional love, then God's work is quietly mediated through human agents to alleviate torment and suffering.

A person who is violated, whether desecrated sexually or otherwise, often experiences a deep sense of filth and contamination. The psalmist's cry, "Create in me a clean heart, O God, and put a new and right spirit within me" (Ps. 51:10), pleads for a renewal, a cleansing that in our day is often communicated in the rite of baptism. Baptism in the name of Jesus cleanses from sin. Some liturgical churches set aside four or five Sundays during the year when the lessons, hymns, prayers, and preaching are used to remind parishioners that the waters of baptism regenerate and give new life.

On regular Sundays the theology and symbolism of baptism may be lurking beneath the "water stories" in the New Testament. Some references are obvious, like the discussion of Jesus with the woman at the well, followed by a discourse on the "water of life" (John 4:7-15). Others are more subtle, such as the healing of the man "blind from birth," which included his washing in the pool of Siloam (John 9). When water or cleansing are primary features in a New Testament narrative, it is likely that the writer has a baptismal link in mind.

A host of contemporary images in art, film, and literature evoke or suggest baptismal themes. In Pat Conroy's *The Prince of Tides*, Tom Wingo shares with a psychiatrist vignettes from his sister's and his own troubled childhood.

> There was one ritual we developed when we were very small that we revealed to not another living soul. Whenever we were hurting or damaged or sad, whenever our parents had punished or beaten us, the three of us would go to the end of the floating dock, dive into the sun-sweet water, then swim out ten yards into the channel and form a circle together by holding hands. We floated together, our hands clasped in a perfect unbreakable circle. I held Savannah's hand and I held Luke's. All of us touched, bound in a ring of flesh and blood and water. Luke would give a signal and all of us would inhale and sink to the bottom of the river, our hands still tightly joined. We would remain on the bottom until one of us squeezed the hands of the others and we would rise together and break the surface in an explosion of sunlight and breath. . . . Diving down, we knew the safety and silence of that motherless, fatherless world; only when our lungs betrayed us did we rise up toward the wreckage. The safe places could only be visited; they could only grant a momentary intuition of sanctuary. The moment always came when we had to return to our real life to face the wounds and grief indigenous to our home by the river.[25]

The safe place of the abused Wingo children was temporary, but baptism is forever. Being immersed into the death and resurrection of Jesus speaks powerfully to the issue of human suffering. While we humans desire to escape violence and other kinds of suffering, God's power in Jesus Christ is expressed in crucified love. Baptism makes a connection between the violence inflicted upon Jesus and the sufferings experienced in the human community. The sign of the cross on the forehead proclaims that link.

Conclusion

In preaching to Mercedes, a violated person, we affirm a person of significance and value in the eyes of God. Violence may render Mercedes and others like her powerless and mute, so they must have someone who will speak for them, not by naming the name of their distress but by recognizing the depth of their suffering.

Pastor-preachers, speaking obliquely, are able to speak *for* them as well as *to* them. The psalms provide a language of lament. Biblical stories like the story of the woman who was a sinner and the story of the good Samaritan give authority to the message while enabling victims to overhear the gospel. Vignettes from life and literature add picture language to give the message contemporary claim. Liturgical actions like baptism and the rites of confession and forgiveness allow the message of cleansing and healing to reverberate in the assembly of believers.

8

Preaching to Believers
Who Are Fearful

TUESDAY, SEPTEMBER 11, 2001, NEEDS NO INTRODUCTION. All Americans know that on that day the impossible happened. Terrorists turned our own civilian planes against us and struck and destroyed the twin towers of the World Trade Center. Thousands of innocent people perished, and thousands more were left to mourn the loss.

Our national and personal reaction to the catastrophe was multidimensional. One of our primary reactions, and the one that our public officials tried to address immediately, was fear—fear for ourselves, for our loved ones, for our society, and for our future. The reasoning was that if our fear got out of hand, it would become a weapon in our enemies' arsenals.

"There is nothing to fear except fear itself." These Rooseveltian words were not quoted often, but the message they contain was a critical concern to our leaders. "Why is fear to be feared?" An answer to this question will help us understand both the positive and the negative nature of fear and why it must be addressed by our pastoral preaching when it infects our parishioners.

We can begin by distinguishing between fear and anxiety In his classic study *The Meaning of Anxiety*, Rollo May says that unlike anxiety fear has an object, that is, it is prompted by a threat that is definite and definable, allowing us at least theoretically to get out of its way. In distinction, anxiety has no locatable object. It represents an attack on "the core or essence of the personality,"[1] that is, on values on which we build our identity and security. We cannot step outside of it or take immediate action against it.

Applied to our reaction to the New York tragedy, the distinction means that we experienced both fear and anxiety, the one leading to the other. Initially we experienced fear. The threat was identifiable;

the target of the attacks could be located temporally and spatially. Quickly our fear tended to "spread out" so that we began to fear many other potential threats, including the threat that each of us represented to the other. As we reacted with fear, the threat burrowed more deeply into our consciousness. Soon it was not just an attack on our buildings but on our way of life and on the values we cherish. Life itself suddenly became problematic, and we were threatened with an impending sense of doom. We were experiencing anxiety.

The path between fear and anxiety is not automatic, nor is it just one-way. As we have indicated, fear can lead to anxiety, but the reverse is also true. Anxiety can lead to fear or, more precisely, we can turn anxiety into fear, mostly to make it more manageable. If our anxiety is experienced as fear, we can avoid the object that is feared, or at least we can control, or adjust to, the object easier. Sigmund Freud gave expression to this insight in his concept of phobia. The individual develops an exaggerated and often an inexplicable aversion to some object in his or her world and then tries to avoid that object. The underlying anxiety is silenced; the feared object is managed.

In our discussion of believers who are fearful, we need to be mindful of the possibility that there is anxiety underneath, but we will focus primarily on the dynamics of fear itself. We can begin by sketching a concrete case of it.

Wanda Wiggins was one hundred miles from the World Trade Center when it collapsed on September 11. She first heard about the tragedy from a friend who was listening to a car radio that morning. Immediately, Wanda turned on the television set and followed the unfolding events until she went to bed late that night.

Wanda woke up the next morning with great apprehension about a forthcoming trip to a professional meeting. Because she was scheduled to give a paper at the meeting, she had made plane reservations a month and a half earlier. The meeting was three weeks away, early in October. Her immediate impulse was to cancel the trip, but she knew that her appearance and her presentation at the meeting were critical to her career. When the ban on commercial flights was lifted by the FAA, Wanda spent the day trying to call the airline. She wasn't sure what she was going to ask them, but she thought it would help to talk to someone about her flight. She got a busy signal all day and into the night. She went to bed angry and apprehensive even though she knew she was not going to get on that plane.

Wanda lived with the apprehension for a week and then decided to call her best friend, a woman her age who had been a dependable support in previous crises. When Wanda started to talk about the tragedy in New York, her friend also registered concern and grief. Wanda was testing "the waters," and when she was convinced that her friend would help, she asked her to drive her to the meeting. The friend, though concerned about flying, was not "scared to death" of it. She urged Wanda to keep the plane reservations and fly to the meeting. Wanda hid the depth of her fear and got off the phone as quickly as she could.

A few days later Wanda received a letter from the chair of the meeting confirming the time of her presentation and welcoming her as a participant. Wanda was glad that she had not canceled the plane reservations, but when she actually thought of getting on the plane, she saw it crashing into the Sears Tower. She went to her computer and opened Rand McNally's Tripmaker. She was surprised to find that the meeting was 420 miles away. She hated to drive that distance, but it was better than being on an ill-fated plane.

The meeting was now three days away, and Wanda still had her plane reservations. She began to put things aside for the trip but could not put them in a suitcase. The night before the trip she called the airline, and when she did not like the "sound" of the man on the other end, she canceled her reservation. By that time it was too late to make the trip by car, so there was no need to start out the next morning. She went to bed and cried herself to sleep.

Wanda's situation indicates that there are at least three consequences of being filled with fear. Each one represents a challenge to pastoral ministry.

The Fruits of Fear

Being Constantly on Guard

As a reaction to an identifiable threat, fear prepares the body to deal with it. It sets in motion what Walter B. Cannon calls the "flight-fight mechanism."[2] The heart beats faster. The peripheral blood vessels contract. Breathing becomes deeper and more rapid. The pupils of the eyes dilate. The liver releases sugar to provide increased energy. Digestive activity is suspended, and the individual experiences the urge to empty bladder and bowels. All these changes are automatic reactions of the body, equipping it either to confront the threat or to get out of its way.

Obviously, this state of preparedness serves a good and necessary purpose in relation to immediate threats. Anything less would impair the person's ability to meet the challenge. But if, as in Wanda's case, the threat continues over an indefinite period of time and the body remains in constant readiness, the individual gradually wears down or even wears out. Physically, the person can experience headache, nausea, sore throat, fever, dizziness, and lingering fatigue—all signs of a decreased capacity to cope with the trouble. Psychologically, the person can become insensitive to the danger. He or she hears "Wolf, wolf" once too often and turns a deaf ear to the warnings, even if the warnings have an air of authenticity about them. Wanda eventually got to the point of relative indifference, first in terms of the possibility of more terrorist attacks and then in terms of the frenzy created by the anthrax invasion. But for her the toll was not that she became callused to the warnings and fell victim to the danger but that she could not find an effective way to live in a world of insecurity. She continued to retreat from the demands of her job, especially when it involved travel, even while she lived in a heightened state of mobilization.

Living in a Narrow World

Persons who live in fear live in a narrowed-down world. Life is restricted in some significant way, which means that certain possibilities are not available to the individual. Of course, under certain circumstances or at certain times the individual may want to, or even need to, restrict his or her options or behaviors, but these restrictions should not be imposed in a premature or absolute way. The people who were devastated by the tragedy in New York may experience legitimate fears related to it, including the fear that the tragedy could be duplicated in other times and places. In this case, fear is a realistic reaction to an actual or impending threat, and it may save us from walking into harm's way. But if this fear continues far beyond any imminent or real danger or if it becomes an absolute or unexamined restriction on our activity, it narrows our world and cuts off possibilities indiscriminately, that is, without regard to their merit or value. In this sense, living in fear is a premature and often an artificial limitation on life. It precludes genuine freedom and fulfillment.

Wanda took her first full step into this fear-bound world when she failed to go to her meeting. The damage she did to her career when she did not show up for her presentation was not insignificant, but even more significant was what fear did to her attitude and outlook toward life in general. She became preoccupied with the possibility of the unpredictable and spent so much time trying to avoid various threats that she failed to respond to the opportunities that were available to her. Of course, the process of living itself involves cutting away possibilities for the sake of direction and focus, but a fear-bound life is a confining bivouac. It represents a retreat into a narrow world to maintain some semblance of security.

If the object we fear is a person, there are secondary consequences, not least of which is anger and even hatred toward the person who threatens us. Actually, anyone or anything that constricts our world may arouse our anger, even if we have done it primarily to ourselves. In this sense fear, like anxiety, is disjunctive. It breaks our relationship with others and drives us toward seclusion. This consequence was expressed in Wanda's reaction to her friend when the friend refused to drive her to her meeting. Wanda got off the phone as soon as she could, not just to hide the depth of her fear but also to express the anger and alienation that she felt toward the friend.

The situation is aggravated because fear also raises the issue of trust. It shows that someone or something has proven to be an imminent threat rather than a dependable ally. Sometimes the very thing we trust the most turns out to be most untrustworthy. Thus fear leads to the question "In whom or in what can we trust?" Wanda did not ask this question explicitly, but her actions gave her away. On two different occasions, she called the airline looking for reassurance from the very agency that was part of the problem. She was not reassured.

Fearing the Penultimate More than the Ultimate

Fear has a way of fixing the mind on the present, on what is an immediate concern or danger. There is a realism in this orientation, for there is a definite threat, and that threat exists in the person's contemporary world. In this sense, Wanda's fear is realistic and should be taken seriously.

At the same time, fear has a tendency to distort our perspective on life. It demands that we give attention to our surroundings, and while this may be necessary in the present moment, it may preclude a wider grasp of the situation. This fact is portrayed in the body's preparation to fight or flee. The pupils of the eyes dilate to give us a better view of the danger, but as we focus on the danger, we are oblivious to the wider world. Wanda is a case in point. On September 11 she spent all day looking at the tragedy on television. In the following days and weeks, she became preoccupied with the unfolding drama and could not give her mind fully to anything else.

Wanda's experience can be used to point to a greater truth. Fear tends to focus the mind on penultimate concerns to the neglect of ultimate concerns. Or to put it another way, a person in Wanda's situation is living by fear and not by faith, even though that person may long to be reassured by an ultimate power. A radical change is in order. A look at the biblical understanding of fear will clarify the point.

From a biblical perspective, fearing the penultimate rather than the ultimate elevates the relative over the absolute, the secondary over the essential. "Do not fear those who kill the body but cannot kill the soul; rather fear [God] who can destroy both soul and body in hell" (Matt. 10:28). We find the same refrain in the Lord's words to Ahaz, king of Judah, "Do not fear what [this people] fears, or be in dread. But the LORD of hosts, him you shall regard as holy; let him be your fear, and let him be your dread" (Isa. 8:12b-13).

To fear the Lord is not just a change in the object we fear; it is a different kind of orientation. According to Scripture, the worldly fear that we have been talking about is marked by timidity, lack of courage, and even paralysis. Fear of God is a bold response to the holy and the merciful, a response that both repels and attracts.

It repels. It is being in the presence of God, the almighty one, and experiencing awe and even terror. It is recognizing God's power and rightness and being acutely aware of one's humble status. This reaction is accentuated if the sinner is aware of his or her sin. Like Adam and Eve who feared God after their act of disobedience, the sinner trembles, shudders in anticipation of God's chastising retribution.

Fear of God also attracts. It perceives God's glory and grasps "God's intense concern and love for man."[3] It is a joyous response to God's saving work in Christ. In this sense, the fear of God is a fruit of faith and is always related to the love of God. This love, if perfected in us, "casts out fear" (1 John 4:18), partly in relation to the dangers of this world but certainly in relation to the retribution of God.

Wanda feared, but her fear was a worldly fear. Without minimizing her fear, pastoral preaching must help her find a fear that takes away all fear.

Preaching to Wanda

Preaching to Wanda may occur, and ideally should occur, within a pastoral relationship. Wanda may not like being paralyzed by fear and may come in to talk to the pastor. Whether she actually takes that step or not, hopefully she sees her pastor as a possible resource of help and care.

If Wanda comes in, she should be encouraged to talk about the entire experience of September 11 and its attendant emotions. She may begin with an objective description of her struggle, but she needs to be helped to get to the subjective world in which her fear thrives. As she tells her story and draws strength from the pastor's empathy, images may be sharpened, dangers clarified, and confidence restored.

In addition to whatever benefit Wanda may get from pastoral counseling, she needs to be addressed on Sunday morning by the proclaimed word. The pastor can assume that Wanda is not the only needy one in the congregation. The events of September 11 probably had a significant impact on most members of the congregation, with many of them experiencing some degree of fear. They may even share a number of common reactions to the tragedy, like staying close to home, being obsessed with the latest news, experiencing nights of restless sleep, canceling scheduled trips, and forgoing planned vacations. Thus the preacher can safely address the issue of fear without being concerned that Wanda will feel singled out and exposed.

The pastor may choose to tell his or her own story of fear as part of the sermon. If Wanda sees the tragedy through the preacher's eyes and identifies with the pastor's feelings, she may get in touch with her own feelings and be empowered to move beyond her own narrow concerns. She may even be helped to see the event from a different angle.

To be sure, there are dangers in the pastor's sharing. The preacher's story may sound padded and contrived to people who are immersed in their own reactions. Or the pastor may get caught up in his or her own experience and become overwhelmed by feelings. In that case, sharing breaches the bonds of modesty and becomes excessive. If this happens, communication suffers as listeners are taken from their own story and become concerned about the preacher. Nevertheless, it remains true that the preacher's restrained but honest reaction to a common event often assists listeners. If done with care and sensitivity, the pastor's story provides a fresh and often an insightful point of view. Edgar Jackson once spoke of this as "a healing perspective."[4]

> If we understand the function of worship as a sanity-restoring and health-creating activity of the Spirit, we see the place of preaching as a part of it in a different light. Then the words of the preacher are not independent of the service of worship, but are a part of its perspective-giving, . . . and insight-creating discipline.[5]

The pastoral preacher has an opportunity to move the sermon, and therefore the congregation, from raw emotions to crucial questions, particularly to questions that have theological import. The pastor might say:

> As I sat in front of the television set, hour after hour, mesmerized by repeated pictures of the second plane hitting its target and terrified people being chased down the streets by clouds of flying debris, I found myself asking: Why did this happen? What could we have done to deserve it? Has God abandoned us?

Difficult questions on the preacher's lips may make it easier for Wanda and others to acknowledge their own laments and questions. In preaching to fearful people, though, the temptation to reassure may become overwhelming. In the face of adversity, most people want quick answers to paralyzing fears. Instead of providing easy answers, which in the long run may prove superficial and misleading, the concerned pastor should acknowledge the hard questions. Instead of protecting people from threatening issues, the pastor should allow them to feel the threat in order to stimulate reflection and, hopefully, adaptation. Instead of denying problems, the pastor should face them head-on so that values can be clarified and attitudes changed.

In previous chapters we spoke about the importance of images as a key strategy for communicating emotions and permitting reality to reach reflection. For suffering believers images express existential realities more effectively than abstract statements, for they can be immediate, personal, and concrete. The most effective kind of image for preaching to Wanda and others is a picture language that portrays the dilemma while pointing to a better way. In a sermon preached in the chapel of the Lutheran Theological Seminary at Philadelphia, then President John W. Vannorsdall used picture language to show how fear limited his vision.[6]

> I was splitting logs behind my house in Vermont when the call came that an elderly neighbor's chimney was blocked and help was needed. Getting the extension ladder from the garage, the two of us set it firmly against the house. Then taking a rope, to which was attached a cinder block for lowering into the chimney, I began climbing to the roof, some forty feet above the ground.
>
> Getting from the ladder to the roof surface was the most frightening part. It was especially tricky carrying both rope and cinder block. Mounting the roof, I groped my way to the peak, edged over to the chimney, and embraced it. When the cinder block had been let down and the chimney was open again, I carefully but hurriedly returned to earth.
>
> "How was the view up there?" asked the neighbor.
>
> "View?" I snapped back. "All I saw were gray shingles, red bricks, and a black hole." Hanging on for dear life, I was oblivious to the view—a New England autumn, woods and sparkling lake, a brilliantly colored world.

Vannorsdall points to the importance of "a view from the roof" for people who are focused on shingles, bricks, and a black hole. The Bible provides a hopeful perspective for myopic believers, for it envisions a time when God will come to rescue.

Strengthen the weak hands,
and make firm the feeble knees.
Say to those who are of a fearful heart,
"Be strong, do not fear!
Here is your God
He will come with vengeance,
with terrible recompense.
He will come and save you." (Isa. 35:3-4)[7]

To the Hebrews who were imprisoned in Babylon and sunk in despair, a voice cried out what God was about to do:

"In the wilderness prepare the way of the LORD,
make straight in the desert a highway for our God.
Every valley shall be lifted up,
and every mountain and hill be made low;
the uneven ground shall become level,
and the rough places a plain.
Then the glory of the LORD shall be revealed,
and all people shall see it together,
for the mouth of the LORD has spoken." (Isa. 40:3-5)

From the peak of the roof, the prophet envisions a road-building project and safe passage for exiles heading home. While such images of ultimate promise may seem far removed from the reality of daily life, they do project God's vision for us and for our world. Our challenges are not removed, but in the midst of this frightening world, we can say "the glory of the LORD shall be revealed." God has the last word. Our Deliverer has spoken, so with confidence we can "say to those who are of a fearful heart, 'Be strong, do not fear!' "

Preaching to Fear Generally

In her short story "The Geranium," Flannery O'Connor tells the story of Dudley and his favorite plant.[8] Each day old Dudley sat in his chair by a window and looked across the alley to another window in an adjacent building. The people who lived there, who Dudley did not know, put out a geranium plant every morning about 10:00 and took it in about 5:30. With little else to concern him, Dudley was often agitated because these careless people set the plant on the edge of the windowsill where the wind could blow it off.

One day the geranium was not there. Instead, sitting in the window was a man in an undershirt. When Dudley asked about the geranium, the man turned hostile. "It fell off if it's any of your business." Dudley looked. Sure enough, six floors down he saw "a cracked flower pot scattered over a spray of dirt and something pink sticking out of a green paper bow."[9] The plant was smashed.

Dudley wanted to go down and retrieve the geranium, but even as he approached the hallway, with its dark and steep stairs, he became fearful and returned to his apartment. The geranium remained "at the bottom of the alley with its roots in the air."

After September 11 the twin towers and the hopes of an entire nation lay splattered on the ground, "roots in the air." In Philadelphia a commentator wrote:

> My first reaction? Fear that this could be the first of many attacks, perhaps in a number of cities. Fear, not for myself, but for our children, recently departed for school.
>
> Everyone felt that clutch of fear. That was the intent of the attacks.[10]

In the wake of September 11, films like *Black Sunday,* in which FBI and Israeli forces foil terrorists who hijack the Goodyear blimp and plan to crash it into the Super Bowl crowd before kickoff, seem naïve. More realistic is *The Siege,* in which a response to Arab terrorists results in the imposition of martial law in Manhattan, with innocent citizens confined in concentration camps. Suddenly library and bookstore shelves emptied as readers were drawn to Nelson DeMille's novel, *The Lion's Game,* the story of an Arab terrorist, Asad Khalil, who left a trail of smoke and blood across the United States.

People living in a fear-narrowed world may appreciate the image of Ernest Campbell, who decades ago preached a sermon with the suggestive title "Locked in a Room with Open Doors."[11] Campbell's thesis was that some people who are technically open and available to others can become closed human beings. Fear causes them to become trapped inside, preoccupied with threats real and imagined and unable to reach out to share and to love.

Not just individuals but groups of people, organizations, and even Christian congregations can be locked in with all the doors open. On the one hand, the welcome sign is out; on the other hand, fear and self-centeredness combine to secure the entry. Strangers are not extended hospitality, and the central task of the congregation, taking the good news of Jesus Christ in word and deed to the world, is thwarted by fear.

How can fear be overcome? How can individuals and organizations break the invisible bonds that lock them in?

Much of what we have written earlier about courage (see chapter 6, pp. 79–81) is applicable here. In addition, it is wise to remember that Christianity does not provide the church and its leaders with pat answers as much as it helps us to raise and wrestle with critical questions. It gives us a way to think about and to live courageously with questions that emerge out of human suffering.

The tradition known as the "theology of the cross" is helpful to us. It is bold enough to confront negative human experiences like pain, fear, and failure. Contrary to those who claim that suffering is illusory, it asserts that suffering is real. "All people are grass . . . the grass withers, the flower fades" (Isa. 40:6-7). Simultaneously, the theology of the cross affirms that suffering is not the final word about our human condition. God is with us in suffering and is able to inspirit us with faith, hope, and courage, even in our darkest hour.

The Power of Stories

In addressing believers who are fearful, the preacher should not overlook the power of hope-filled stories—stories of courage in the face of fear, stories of caring and being cared for in an otherwise menacing world.

In the aftermath of the destruction of the World Trade Center, primary attention was centered on the actions of police, firefighters, and EMTs. Behind the scenes, ordinary Americans began to line up to donate blood. Acts of courage and heroism began to appear. Young office workers helped older colleagues to safety. Disabled persons were carried down stairways in chairs. People died as they rushed back into the towers to rescue friends left behind. A Roman Catholic priest was crushed while administering last rites. Telling and retelling these stories of heroism and compassion focuses the mind on the miracle of care in the midst of chaos, helping the fearful to live with some degree of hope.

The Power of Music

Music is also an antidote to fear or loss of hope. Since the September 11 tragedy, Americans have rediscovered the healing power of music. Pop songs like "One More Day" and "Love Can Build a Bridge" have provided precious moments of relief from fear. And "God Bless America" has become the "hymn of the day" for American civil religion. Its composer, Irving Berlin, wrote the song as a bid for peace when war threatened Europe in 1938. Recently, at a memorial service at the National Cathedral in Washington, D.C., the song was used as a national prayer.

Pastoral preachers will be well advised to use hymns of the church as preaching texts or as hopeful images in sermons. If familiar hymns are used, the listener's mind and heart are immediately engaged. In the hymn "O God, Our Help in Ages Past,"[12] Isaac Watts paraphrases Psalm 90 and evokes hope in believers. Without using the word *fear,* he acknowledges what is most fearful, death, and places the believer under the shadow of God's throne, there to dwell secure.

> O God, our help in ages past,
> Our hope for years to come,
> Our shelter from the stormy blast,
> And our eternal home.
>
> Under the shadow of your throne
> Your saints have dwelt secure;
> Sufficient is your arm alone,
> And our defense is sure.
>
> Time, like an ever-rolling stream,
> Soon bears us all away,
> We fly forgotten, as a dream
> Dies at the opening day.
>
> O God, our help in ages past,
> Our hope for years to come,
> Still be our guard while troubles last
> And our eternal home! (*Lutheran Book of Worship,* 320)

The singing of this hymn, or the humming of it in the mind, can recall God's gracious activity in the past. At the same time, it reminds us of God's sure defense in the here-and-now even as it affirms that God is "our hope for years to come."

Martin Luther too has given us a hymn of strength and consolation. Since Vatican II, "A Mighty Fortress Is Our God" has reached across Protestant and Roman Catholic lines to bring comfort to all suffering Christians.

> Though hordes of devils fill the land
> All threatening to devour us
> We tremble not, unmoved we stand;
> They cannot overpower us.
> Let this world's tyrant rage;
> In battle we'll engage!
> His might is doomed to fail;
> God's judgment must prevail!
> One little word subdues him. (*Lutheran Book of Worship*, 229)

Michael Joncas's "On Eagles' Wings" has been played repeatedly on radio since September 11. It is a musical setting of Psalm 91 with related images from texts like Isaiah 40:31. The version sung by Michael Crawford has become a special source of strength for fearful persons.[13]

> You who dwell in the shelter of the Lord,
> who abide in his shadow for life,
> Say to the Lord: "My refuge,
> my rock in whom I trust!"
>
> And he will raise you up on eagle's wings,
> bear you on the breath of dawn,
> make you to shine like the sun,
> and hold you in the palm of his hand.[14]

"Leaning on the Everlasting Arms" is another hymn of reassurance.

> What have I to dread, what have I to fear,
> leaning on the everlasting arms!
> I have blessed peace with my Lord so near,
> leaning on the everlasting arms.
>
> Leaning, leaning, safe and secure from all alarms;
> Leaning, leaning, leaning on the everlasting arms.[15]

The corpus of African American spirituals contains many songs that have inspired suffering people. Composed in the midst of suffering, songs like the following are keyed to biblical texts that are appropriate for fearful believers.

"My Lord, What a Morning"
"There Is a Balm in Gilead"
"When Israel Was in Egypt's Land"
"I Want Jesus to Walk with Me"
"In the Morning When I Rise"

Conclusion

Wanda is an example of how fear can create a narrowed-down world. Persons who ordinarily are open to constructive interaction are driven toward seclusion. Theologically, fear upsets the priorities of persons or even of congregations by replacing proper respect for God's power and glory with worldly concerns.

The terrorist acts of September 11 make it clear that fear is a social and not just an individual phenomenon. Significant events in the world "out there" are internalized, filling individuals like Wanda with fear. But these events also yield images of the world—fiery explosions, body bags, and crumbled towers. The pastoral preacher must address those who live in this terrifying world, helping them to see through darkened glass.

In the face of fear, narratives of courage strengthen Christians. If used in sermons, stories of courage, particularly contemporary stories from the pages of daily newspapers, have power to reassure. Songs and hymns also bring hope to many. They can serve as a channel for God to enter into and transform human lives. They can make real to the fearful Paul's benediction to the Romans: "May the God of hope fill you with all joy and peace in believing, so that you may abound in hope by the power of the Holy Spirit" (Rom. 15:13).

9

Preaching to Believers Who Experience Failure

Willy Loman, a sixty-year-old salesman in Arthur Miller's *Death of a Salesman,*[1] bets his life on the belief that success is achievable if one is pleasant to and well-liked by potential customers. With a show of pride, he says to his two sons, Biff and Happy: "They know me, boys, they know me up and down New England. . . . I can park my car in any street in New England, and the cops protect it like their own."[2] Later in the play, when Willy defends himself against Biff 's supposed insult, he reassures himself: "Go to Filene's, go to the Hub, go to Slottery's, Boston. Call out the name of Willy Loman and see what happens! Big shot!"[3]

Willy has caught the American dream. He believes that if you exemplify clean living, industry, and thrift, you will get ahead and land near the top. This dream allows no room for failure, no recognition of uncertainty, let alone frailty and brokenness. Yet Willy Loman cannot silence the other side. He brags about being "very well liked in Hartford," and in the same breath he says to his wife, "You know, the trouble is, Linda, people don't seem to take to me."[4] Later when he is at the mercy of his boss, he pleads, "I put thirty-four years into this firm, Howard, and now I can't pay my insurance! You can't eat the orange and throw the peel away—a man is not a piece of fruit!"[5]

Willy Loman confronts us with the reality of human failure, but we really do not need his reminder. Our own lives are a witness to the fact that the American dream of unambiguous success and self-confidence is not really real. As Paul Tillich says: "There is only one alternative to life with failure [and] that is lifelessness without failure."[6]

The Sources of Failure

A sense of failure can be a crippling judgment on the self. It can haunt our moments of greatest success and make us feel that we have achieved nothing. It can linger in the shadows of our lives and erode our self-confidence whenever it wants to. How do we account for such a devastating development? Willy Loman indicates that there are at least three reasons why we can fail.

First, we may fail because of the social and historical forces that act upon us. We may live in situations and work under circumstances that preclude success, at least in the way or to the degree that we hope. Willy may not be the smash in New England that he imagines, because New England merchants may not like to undercut local business people by buying from "foreign" salesmen. Of course the obstacles to his success may run much deeper. They may include the many determinants that make Willy the kind of person he is, or they may have something to do with the contingent and unpredictable nature of human existence itself. In any case, these many forces are symbolized in Miller's play by the tall structures that overshadow Willy's house and make it impossible for him "to see a star in this yard"[7] unless he looks straight up.

How Willy responds to these contextual forces is important. By his attitude he can soften their impact, even though he cannot eliminate these forces. They represent a context of determinants that may nudge him toward failure without his being an active agent in its actualization. He lives, as we do, in a society and in an era in which failure may come in spite of our best attempts to succeed.

Second, we can fail because we are limited and finite creatures. We can will one thing and not have the ability to carry it out. We can foresee certain consequences and be hit by unanticipated developments. We can imagine the impossible but do not have the power to actualize it. Most of all, we are heirs of immortality but walk with feet of clay—on the treadmill toward death.

Willy is sixty years old and approaching retirement. He is too old to make the long trip to his New England territory and goes to his boss to see if he can be assigned to the home office. The boss will not consider or cater to his age and infirmities. In fact, he uses them to fire Willy, robbing him of all dignity and plunging him into a finale of failure.

Combined with the social and historical forces that act upon us, our finite limitations are often an active ingredient in our struggle with failure. Again, how we respond to these realities determines, in part, the role they play in our lives. The more we deny our creature-liness, the more it may determine us, if not in an obvious way, then certainly by the drag it puts on our fondest dreams. In any case, to be human is to be finite, and to be finite is to be acquainted with defeat. Third, we may fail because we program ourselves to fail. This is the most paradoxical and tragic source of human failure. We can use the personality theory of Karen Horney to illuminate its dynamics.[8]

For Horney the basic evil, that is, the most destructive dynamic in human relationships, is the lack of genuine warmth and devotion. When love is not genuine or, what is worse, when a lack of love is camouflaged by sham acts of affection, the person fails to develop a real sense of security, self-esteem, and relatedness. The result is what Horney calls "basic anxiety," which means that the person lives with a basic "feeling of being isolated and helpless in a world conceived as potentially hostile."[9] The individual makes whatever adjustments are necessary to survive in this frightening world, but fundamental needs are left unfulfilled. The need for real self-confidence, the need for genuine relation to others, and the need for a solid sense of identity are all left unsatisfied.

A solution to this dilemma must be found, which means for Horney that over time a basic change occurs in the individual's life. Instead of trying to actualize who one really is, the individual initiates a substitute process of growth that Horney calls a "search for glory." It is an attempt to actualize an "idealized self" rather than the "real self."[10] The attitude of idealization infiltrates the individual's aspirations, goals, conduct of life, and relation to others. The person identifies the self with (literally, equates the self with) what he or she thinks he or she should be rather than with what he or she actually is. This attitudinal change is manifested in every activity and on every level of the personality.

However much individuals try to actualize their idealized selves, Horney continues, they cannot escape reality completely. Both the limitations of their own being and the actualities of life and relationships inevitably remind them that their world has not been ordered totally to accord with the wishes of infinite realization. According to Horney, the individual has two ways to muffle the message of reality: the first one, effective against the demands of the world, is called "neurotic claims"; the second one, effective against the limitations of the self, is called "the tyranny of the should." It is the second maneuver that attracts our attention.

"The tyranny of the should" refers to insatiable inner dictates that operate on the premise "that nothing should be, or is, impossible for oneself."[11] These inner dictates are completely insensitive to the actual conditions under which individuals can find genuine fulfillment. Instead, life revolves around what ought to be, for these people are dominated by the relentless demand that they should be different and more perfect than they really are. They strive to mold themselves into a supreme being of their own making. They hold before themselves the image of perfection and are tortured by what they "should be able to do, to be, to feel, to know."[12] If, for example, they feel that they should be a dominant and powerful person, they decry any sign of weakness. And if they feel that they should be a submissive person, they hate any sign of strength and self-assertion.

It should be clear that the "shoulds" are qualitatively different than genuine ideals, for they are permeated by a spirit of egoism and are dominated by a spirit of coercion. Instead of urging individuals toward the actualization of their real selves, they destroy spontaneous growth, distort relationships with others, and force people to live a life of insatiable demands.

Horney's "tyranny of the should" casts an illuminating light on a sense of failure. It tells us that we can struggle with a sense of failure, not because we have failed to live up to who we are but because we have not measured up to who we think we ought to be.

This means that we can experience a sense of failure precisely when it is not warranted. For example, if we are submissive, self-effacing persons, we will feel like we have failed when we have stood up for ourselves and asserted ourselves. In this case, our sense of failure takes us away from what we may need to do and keeps us in bondage to the idealization process.

The full significance of Horney's theory is not uncovered until we view it from a theological perspective. The idealization process is a way to create ourselves in our own image, to make ourselves acceptable to ourselves and, hopefully, to God. It is a rejection of what we are and a mandate of what we ought to be. Thus it gives us the appearance of living a moral and meritorious life, especially since any failure to live up to our high standards subjects us to an incriminating sense of self-condemnation. In a sense, we win both ways. We strive to be "good," but if we fail to live up to our high standards, we still win because our intentions are good, and we will strive to do better the next time. In another sense, we do not win at all. We fall sorrowfully short of what we should be and struggle with guilt and failure.

A life of insatiable demands is an endless search for perfection. It actually tends to increase rather than decrease our feeling of not measuring up. Any failure, no matter how small, brings with it harsh judgment. More important, a life of tyrannical demands goes beyond the attempt to make oneself acceptable and is actually a destructive and boundless pursuit of false fulfillment. In the language of Horney, it is a denial of the real self and an attempt to mold one's finite life into infinite goodness. In Paul's language it is zeal for the law, for it holds the law of our own making in high regard and puts our trust in our compulsive attempt to keep it. In actual fact, it is a futile exercise in self-righteousness, for it attempts to make us acceptable by being the ultimate actualization of a self-defined and impossible perfection. In the end, it is an idolatrous house of cards that collapses under the weight of an oppressive sense of failure.

The Facets of Failure

A Sense of Incompetence

In a society that emphasizes success, one must be competent—not just run-of-the-mill competent but well-above-average competent. A series of minor failures may not reflect on our competence, but frequent failures begin to erode any sense of adequacy, first as a momentary reflection on the self and then eventually as a permanent attitude toward and evaluation of the self. Then even if we are successful, we may feel incompetent by reason of our own self-evaluation. This whole cycle is accentuated if we are judging ourselves by idealized "shoulds" that are too demanding ever to be fulfilled.

Willy struggles with a sense of inadequacy, and it gets reinforced every time he goes out on a selling trip. After he returns from New England, Linda, his wife, asks him, "Did you sell anything?"

"Five hundred gross in Providence and seven hundred in Boston," Willy replies. The figures are soon revised. "Well, I—I did—about a hundred and eighty gross in Providence. Well, no—it came to—roughly two hundred gross on the whole trip."[13] Then Willy aggravates his own sense of failure by asking Linda, "What do we owe?" After a litany of bills and expenses, Willy soothes his sense of incompetence by saying, "Oh, I'll knock 'em dead next week."[14]

Later Willy puts his idealized demands on Biff and lives through him. He pushes Biff to ask for a big starting salary, as he is about to meet a prospective employer. "Start big and you'll end big."[15] Willy may be trying to encourage himself as much as he is Biff when he adds, "You got greatness in you, Biff; remember that. You got all kinds a greatness."[16] The assertion of greatness may not quell the sense of incompetence. In fact, it may increase it.

A Sense of Worthlessness

In a society that prizes performance, the individual who fails experiences a sense of worthlessness. The inability to measure up reflects back on one's self-esteem, partly because one has failed in one's own eyes and partly because one's inadequacy is reflected in the reaction and evaluations of others.

Biff's journey in the play serves as an illustration. He starts out as a high school star, the best on the football team. In the pomp of his popularity, he fails a math course, and contrary to his expectations, Mr. Birnhaum, the teacher, refuses to change the grade. Devastated, Biff travels to Boston to see his father and discovers that his father is having an affair with Miss Francis, a buyer. Biff is inconsolable, wrenches himself from his father, and refuses to take a summer course that would allow him to graduate. His sense of worth is battered still more by subsequent events: He is caught stealing and is put in prison for three months, he cannot hold or get a decent job, he cannot get himself together. Gradually, he is brought to the brink of grim self-assessment: "I am not a leader of men, Willy, and neither are you. . . . Pop, I'm nothing! I'm nothing, Pop. Can't you understand that? There's no spite in it any more. I'm just what I am, that's all."[17]

Biff's confession is both an honest acknowledgment of how he has come to see himself and a sad expression of his struggle with failure. The one leads to the other. The endpoint of low self-esteem is a life of failure, and a life of failure leads to increased self-deprecation. Horney's insatiable demands add a note of futility to the process. No matter how successful the individual may be, he or she falls short of perfection. The consequent sense of worthlessness can be deadly.

A Sense of Shame

In chapter 7 we talked about being shamed, about a failure or a failing being exposed when we did not want it to show. It should not surprise us, then, to discover that shame is an inherent part of our present discussion.

Shame is often more covert than overt mostly because, like anxiety, it involves the whole self and wipes away the ground on which we stand. "Coming suddenly upon us, experiences of shame throw a flooding light on what and who we are."[18] Our hiding place is gone. To make matters worse, given the holistic nature of shame, "shame can be altered or transcended only in so far as there is some change in the whole self. No single, specific thing we can do can rectify or mitigate such an experience."[19] No wonder we take great pains not to experience shame. In fact, not to experience it is a way to retain some sense of self-respect, some sense of competence and worthwhileness. Shame may have the positive intent of urging us to address what is wrong with the self, but in truth it blinds and paralyzes with its piercing light.

Willy's sense of shame lingers just below the surface on many occasions in the play. When he finally confesses to Linda that he only did "roughly two hundred gross on the whole trip,"[20] he retreats from the implied shame by offering an excuse: "The trouble was that three of the stores were half closed for inventory in Boston. Otherwise, I woulda broke records."[21] Linda adds more salve to Willy's wound by saying of his sales, "Well, it makes seventy dollars and some pennies [in commissions]. That's very good."[22]

Throughout the play, Willy struggles with the menacing clouds of shame, but the darkest cloud appears when he is fired and goes to meet his sons for dinner. He confesses to them that he has lost his job even as Biff accentuates the father's shame by telling him that he stole a pen from Mr. Oliver, the prospective employer. The scene ends when the boys abandon their father to spend a night on the town with two pick-up girls. Later at home, Linda bears her husband's shame and tries to make the boys feel some sense of it: "Don't you care whether he lives or dies?"[23] The ruse does not work, and in exasperation she orders, "Get out of here, both of you, and don't come back! I don't want you tormenting him any more."[24] Biff begins to feel the shame. When Linda calls him a louse, he partly confesses and partly derides her: "Now you hit it on the nose! The scum of the earth, and you're looking at him!"[25]

Preaching to Willy

Willy Loman is not inclined to darken the door of a church, but there are Willys who do. They bring their sense of failure with them and take their usual place in the pew, hoping to be encouraged or comforted. Like Arthur Miller's protagonist, they may live by "wrong dreams" or be hard-working people who land "in the ash can," but they cannot be ignored. They hurt too much for that.

Rereading Willy's story and his struggle with failure may be helpful to the preacher's sermon preparation, but if the parishioner's story parallels Willy's too closely, pastoral discretion precludes the direct use of the story in the sermon. Nevertheless, the story is rich with images and spiced with nuances that describe the plight of those who struggle with failure. These can be lifted out of the story and used to articulate the unexpressed hurts and disappointments of a failed life. Charley, a friend of Willy's, provides a fitting description of Willy's plight as a salesman when Biff, at the gravesite, insists that the man "never knew who he was."

> You don't understand: Willy was a salesman. And for a salesman, there is no rock bottom to the life. He don't put a bolt on a nut, he don't tell you the law or give you medicine. He's a man way out there in the blue, riding on a smile and a shoeshine. And when they start not smiling back—that's an earthquake. And then you get yourself a couple of spots on your hat, and you're finished.[26]

Charley's epitaph provides a fitting description of Willy's occupational hazards, but Willy's struggle with failure may go deeper. As our previous analysis indicates, Willy must come to terms with three possible sources of failure: the vicissitudes of life, the limitations of creatureliness, and the tyranny of shoulds. There are resources to meet each of these challenges. We can begin with God's gift of tomorrow. Each day is a new day, a new beginning. "Life is grace. Sleep is forgiveness. The night absolves. Darkness wipes the slate clean, not spotless to be sure, but clean enough for another day's chalking."[27] Usually we are able to survive our yesterdays, and in the morning we are called back to life again. The broken promises, the unfulfilled dreams, and the unspoken words become possibilities again. Life has a certain measure of grace to it and Willy, setting out for New England, experiences the hope.

But life also has a certain persistence to it. Our yesterdays shape our todays and require us to take an honest look at ourselves—where we have been and where we are going. After waiting six hours, Biff finally catches a glimpse of Mr. Oliver. Oliver snubs him, and in the wake of his departure, Biff gets an honest glance at himself. "I realized what a ridiculous lie my whole life has been. We've been talking in a dream for fifteen years. [I was not a salesman for Oliver.] I was a shipping clerk."[28] Biff goes on to admit that he is nothing, a nobody, and he urges Willy to come to a similar self-assessment. Willy refuses to take an honest look and dies a self-deceived failure.

God gives us the gift of self-assessment, and with it God frees us from the delusions that would bind us. Biff's response to the vicissitudes of life and to the limitations of creatureliness is different than when he would not acknowledge their reality and power. He does not become free of them, but he is able to put them in proper perspective, granting the way in which he has been shaped by them and acknowledging the way in which he has contributed to their power. But most of all, honest self-assessment can free us from our feverish attempt to live by and to fulfill our inordinate demands. The gospel is clear. We are not made acceptable by virtue of our works but by the grace of God. To the end, Happy reflects his father's dream: "It's the only dream you can have—to come out number-one man. He fought it out here, and this is where I'm gonna win it for him."[29] Happy, like his father, is doomed to failure, and he may be crushed by it.

Pastoral ministry has the resources to deal with all of this, but if it does or not depends, in part, on Willy. If Willy comes to his pastor, voicing some of his frustrations and sharing some of his struggles, the pastor may have a chance to change the focus of Willy's life. Pastoral preaching can add the living Word. The Lukan parables

(Luke 15) of mercy provide a glimpse into the heart and intention of God in dealing with human failure. The shepherd does not forget the wandering sheep but leaves the rest of the flock to seek the lost one. In a household where a single coin is precious, the woman does not give up on the lost drachma but sweeps the house diligently until she finds it. And the father of the prodigal son does not forsake his own. He waits patiently until the son with a wrong dream returns and then restores his child to a place at the family table. God's forgiveness and reconciliation are at the heart of God's good news, and they can address and recast human failure.

Preaching to Failure Generally

Human failure is complicated by human pride, which persists even in the lives of the redeemed. The cultural axiom, "If at first you don't succeed, try, try again" is engrained deeply in our psyche. This axiom and others like it suggest that failure is a result of not trying hard enough. The American work ethic tells us, as it told Willy, that the way to succeed is to try even harder. Not even Herculean human efforts, though, can overcome failure when it is a manifestation of sin.

The last time our friend took her Cadillac in for a state inspection, it failed to pass. "I'm sorry ma'am," the inspection officer said. "It's a wonderful car, but rust has eaten through the floor of the trunk. Exhaust fumes are seeping into the passenger compartment, and they are lethal."

As Beatrice told the story, she began to think of a solution. On her way home, she stopped at a craft store and purchased sheets of cardboard, duct tape, and silver spray paint. With great care, Bea made an outline of the trunk and cut a piece of cardboard in that precise shape. After spraying the patch silver, taping it in place, and replacing the trunk's rug, she was ready to try again. She took the car to a second inspection station, and it passed with flying colors.

The final victory, though, was not won. Rust and rot still remained. In all the hidden places where metal was joined to metal, the Cadillac was loaded with trouble. In the end the rust would win, and even now the deadly fumes may seep into the trunk and find a victim.

Sadly, the same is true of sinful human pride. A flimsy patch may cover up trouble, but it will never stop the corrosive power of sin. Failure is inevitable.

The primal story of sin as pride is recorded in Genesis 3, where humans who desire greater knowledge and power than God intended violate boundaries. Similarly, in Genesis 11 people seek to build a city and a tower "with its top in the heavens." They challenge God and try to "make a name" for themselves. In the New Testament, Jesus deals with people who, having an inflated sense of their own importance, take the chief seats at a feast. He observes that they will be humiliated when a truly important person arrives and they are asked to take a lower seat.

Pride has corrosive effects. One way to get at this in preaching is to challenge a contemporary axiom like "If at first you don't succeed, try, try again." The sermon might begin by agreeing with the axiom. Indeed, for people who are lazy, lack direction, or are not fully engaged, "Try, try again" may be excellent advice. American lore is replete with stories of persons who lost everything but made new fortunes, of athletes who were cut by teams only to become all-stars, of persons who failed high school algebra but who became stellar scientists. By clarifying objectives, applying their talents, and working hard, they succeeded.

Having confirmed the axiom, the preacher is able to use Beatrice's story, or one like it, to erode its credibility and to introduce the corrosive effects of pride. Pride is not overcome by human effort but in fact is increased by it. It takes God's good news, that we are saved by grace and not by works, to chart a path out of pride and failure. "If at first you don't succeed, put your life in God's hands," for God overcomes the ravages of failure by showing that in the divine scheme of things failure does not count.

Recast by God's grace, failure can become an opportunity to reassess. Robert Frost, in a poem entitled "On a Tree Fallen across the Road," provides an apt image for the preacher.

> The tree the tempest with a crash of wood
> Throws down in front of us is not to bar
> Our passage to our journey's end for good,
> But just to ask us who we think we are
>
> Insisting always on our own way so.
> She likes to halt us in our runner tracks, . . .[30]

One day we seem to be in the vanguard of whatever it is we do, and then suddenly we find ourselves bringing up the rear. We are not promoted or we are downsized outright or we are cast aside like an orange peel. God is not the cause of such events, but God invites us to take these events as opportunities to rethink the course of our lives and to conform our prideful will to God's will. The history of Israel testifies to the fact that God can turn human failure into a blessing. David falls in love with Bathsheba, wife of Uriah, and orders Uriah to the forefront of the battle so he can possess Bathsheba. God is angry and through Nathan confronts David. David is stopped in his tracks and his life is changed. Out of the union of David and Bathsheba, God raises up King Solomon, who continues the Davidic line and builds a temple for God (1 Chronicles 22).

David's story is part of a larger saga of failure and election. In 587 B.C., when Jerusalem fell to the Babylonians and the Davidic dynasty lost power, the faith of the people was shaken. With the fall of the temple, the royal house, and the nation, the people were moved to theological reflection and reaffirmed Yahweh's commitment to them.

> But now thus says the LORD,
> he who created you, O Jacob,
> he who formed you, O Israel:
> Do not fear, for I have redeemed you;
> I have called you by name, you are mine.
> When you pass through the waters, I will be with you;
> and through the rivers, they shall not overwhelm you;
> when you walk through fire you shall not be burned,
> and the flame shall not consume you.
> For I am the LORD your God,
> the Holy One of Israel, your Savior. (Isa. 43:1-3)

Israel's repeated failure to be a "light to the nations" led to the incarnation of the eternal Word in Jesus of Nazareth. According to Philippians 2:1-11, Jesus was born to put in human flesh (to incarnate) "the final and complete self-humiliation of God in man and in the person of Jesus."[31] He came to die, and when he hung abandoned on the cross and was seen as a failure in the eyes of the world, he had already triumphed and completed his mission (see Mark 15:34, 39).

In a real sense, Jesus' own mission was a failure. His coming to convert Israel failed. "He came to what was his own, and his own people did not accept him" (John 1:11). His agony in Gethsemane and his suffering on the cross were signs of failure, which paradoxically were also manifestations of God's will. God confirmed this by raising Jesus to new life. "Was it not necessary that the Messiah should suffer these things and then enter into his glory?" (Luke 24:26).

Jesus' resurrection from the dead was a new beginning. The risen one confronted his disciples, gave them the greeting of peace, showed them his marked hands and side, and bestowed on them the gift of the Holy Spirit and the ministry of forgiveness. He reclaimed the disciples from failure, commissioned them, and sent them out.

"Peace to you" is a farewell gift of the risen one to his disciples then and now. Peace is to accompany former failures as they set out in mission. Thomas, who was absent when Jesus appeared to the disciples, encountered the risen Christ eight days later, and he too was filled with faith and experienced peace. He confessed, "My Lord and my God!" He was ready for mission.

The resurrection stories indicate that people come to faith in the risen Christ in different ways. In a discussion of this passage, Tom Long[32] quotes Fred Craddock:

> What is clear is that faith is not the same experience for all, neither is it generated for all with the same kind and degree of evidence. For some, faith is born and grows as quietly as a child sleeping on grandmother's lap. For others, faith is a lifetime of wrestling with the angel. Some cannot remember when they did not believe, while others cannot remember anything else, their lives having been shattered and reshaped by decision of faith.[33]

These different ways of coming to faith are played out repeatedly in any congregation. In the story of Thomas, Jesus shifts his attention from the disciples to a larger audience. "Blessed are those who have not seen and yet have come to believe" (John 20:29). Jesus acknowledges that, like Thomas, many of us have suffered through periods of doubt and failure. But in the end, as a gift of God, we come to believe without seeing.

The ascended Christ has left us an empty tomb and a community of faith. We are empowered by the Spirit and gathered in joy and trust around Word and table. We live in Christian hope, not in naïve optimism but in hope against hope that even in the midst of failure God will continue to form and strengthen the church. Christ's commission is sufficient: "As the Father has sent me, so I send you" (John 20:21).

Conclusion

Most of us struggle with a sense of failure, not because we have out-and-out failed but because it is impossible for us to live up to the egoistic demands that we have placed on ourselves. The sin of pride, the wanting to be like God, ensnares us in the tyranny of the should. "I should be liked by everyone." "I should impress the boss with what I know." "I ought to be in control of things at all times." It was an impossible dream of success that destroyed Willy Loman.

The good news is that God seeks out and restores the lost. God reclaims failures like Samson, Joseph, and David to fulfill his promise of salvation. When Jesus' mission appears to end in failure and his disciples run for their lives, Jesus confronts them, restores their faith, and equips them for mission. Today God continues to use persons who are familiar with failure to renew the church. Even in a corrosive culture, by the grace of God, rust is stopped and life is renewed.

10

Samples of Pastoral Preaching

THROUGHOUT THIS BOOK we have tried to remain attentive to the pastor who faces suffering believers and who wants seriously to be pastoral to them. We use "pastoral" in the obvious sense of being concerned about, or being solicitous to, persons in need. We also use it in a deeper sense to mean the pastor's attempt to make God's Word relevant to the needs of suffering believers. This is being pastoral in a true sense, for after all, it is not the pastor's word but God's Word that brings a gracious and comforting message to those who suffer.

This means that the pastor, if equipped with God's Word, can be pastoral in many different ways in and through many different acts and functions of ministry. But in order to serve as a mediator of God's comfort, the pastor must be acquainted with suffering and be able to stand alongside the sufferer. In this sense, the pastor's basic posture toward the sufferer is important, for if the pastor is not genuinely concerned about the sufferer, his or her "pastoral" words will not ring true and will not be an effective witness to God's loving care.

Our primary focus in this book has been on the pastor's attempt to be pastoral in the pulpit. We have examined this ministry from different angles and, hopefully, have illuminated its many dimensions. Now it is time to become concrete, to present and to examine actual instances of pastoral preaching. We offer three different sermons, not because they represent absolute forms to be emulated but because they are serious and provocative examples of how two preachers attempted to preach pastorally. We hope these sermons will invite the reader to examine and refine his or her own pastoral address.

Pastoral preaching is an oral event, which means that sermons are to be heard, not read. Many of the features of the proclaimed word, which include gestures, facial expressions, and tone of voice, cannot be reproduced on the printed page. Nevertheless, the format of the sermons that follow should serve as an indication of how they would be presented as auditory experiences. Words that are intended to be spoken together are clustered often on the same line. Some sentences are incomplete and should be presented as they would be in oral speech. The length of a pause is indicated by traditional punctuation marks (for example, commas and periods) or by the space between thoughts. As we discuss each sermon, we will give additional information related to it. The reader is advised to read aloud the biblical text before each sermon in order to replicate the actual procedure in the worship service.

A Sermon on Anger

Context of the Sermon

The Reverend Robert Hughes is a member of the congregation being addressed—St. John Lutheran Church (ELCA), Ocean City, New Jersey. He was filling in for the pastor who was on an August vacation. Typically, on a summer Sunday, fifteen to thirty visitors, many from the nearby Philadelphia area, swell the worshiping congregation to about 180 people.

In August of 2000 anger-inducing events and angry people seemed to fill the headlines. Philadelphia had a rash of violent encounters. A confrontation between the police and a local criminal had received national attention because of its similarity to the Rodney King affair in Los Angeles several years earlier. The Republican National Convention spawned demonstrations and arrests in the city, and this was reported in both the local and the national media. Anger was in the air.

Design and Development of the Sermon

The sermon's first movement focuses on the contemporary problem of anger, first by naming it and then by bringing it to life by using a collage of images. The repetition of the term *anger* is intentional to effect a kind of resonance. The sermon moves from examples of anger at distant places to anger close to home and finally to anger inside. The preacher's admission of his own anger is to provide a note of levity but also to make it easier for listeners to acknowledge their anger. The misstating of Ephesian's teaching on anger is done intentionally to highlight what the text actually says.

The second movement, the response of faith, begins with a teaching moment. Anger as a constructive emotion is differentiated from anger that may lead to bitterness, resentment, and sin. The counsel of Ephesians—that forgiveness is the desired response to anger—is noted, but the sermon also acknowledges that this response is often difficult for Christians. The good news in the text and in the sermon is that forgiveness begins with God. In Jesus Christ, God forgives anger in humans and thus enables us to forgive one another.

The summary of the sermon's message, the "focus sentence," is "When anger at others becomes corrosive and turns to sin, God's forgiveness of us enables us to forgive and to let go of our anger." The purpose or goal of the sermon, the "function sentence," is "To communicate a biblical understanding of anger and forgiveness."

The Sermon:
"Living with a Short Fuse"
(Based on Ephesians 4:25—5:2)

Anger. The word jumps out at us from today's second lesson. Maybe that's because our world seems filled to overflowing with it. We read about anger daily in our newspapers. Images of anger confront us on television, and some of those images linger.

In Philadelphia, we see angry police beating and kicking a local criminal who had stolen a city vehicle and led officers on a merry chase.

In Philadelphia, we see angry demonstrators dumping trash on city streets, blocking intersections, masked demonstrators sitting on the pavement, arms locked together, surly demonstrators shouting epithets at police.

Local newspapers reported, of the convention protesters, that their issues were all over the place, no one message, no unifying crusade. Their anger bound them together.

Anger in the form of "road rage," as it is often called, can be as near as the car behind or in front of you on today's highways. On the New Jersey Turnpike just recently, one angry driver used his van to run a slow-moving automobile off the road, leaving a young woman injured and another in the car near death.

Of course, we don't have to go to Philadelphia to see anger at work, do we? It was present in the beating administered by three young women to another young woman they were attempting to rob right here on the Ocean City boardwalk several weeks ago.

I saw anger in a local supermarket last week, when an irate shopper engaged in a loud exchange with a clerk about delays over a price check.

Anger is everywhere,
anger is all around,
anger is . . . within us.

I'm a fairly calm person, but I feel anger well up in me from time to time . . .

- when trying to get out of a side street on to Bay Avenue as hordes of sun worshipers are leaving the beach
- when the dripping paint brush falls on the floor and white ceiling paint splatters over colored kitchen appliances
- or, as occurred yesterday, when my computer throws a temper tantrum and an important file is lost (this sermon).

For most of us, anger is never far away, is it? Anger lurks beneath the surface, poised, ready to emerge when a crack develops in our cool exterior.

Anger is also a cause of many of the crimes committed by human beings against each other. Psychologists estimate that anger is at the root of 70 to 80 percent of the problems for which people seek professional help.

Because it is a universal human problem, anger was an issue for first-century Christians in the church at Ephesus. The people addressed in today's second lesson were new believers. Like us, like believers in every age, they needed to know what it meant to live as Christians day to day. So what we find in chapter 4 is a catechetical lesson for Ephesians and now, by extension, for us as well.

And Paul's injunctions about living the life of faith are practical and straightforward:

- Don't lie, speak the truth
- Give up stealing, be honest
- Share what you have with the needy, and
- DON'T GET ANGRY.

DON'T GET ANGRY? Is that really what the Letter to the Ephesians says about anger? If you were listening carefully to the reading, you know that it is *not*.

Paul writes:
> Be angry but do not sin;
> do not let the sun go down on your anger,
> and do not make room for the devil.

"Be angry but do not sin." What does that mean? Is it okay to be angry? I'll wager that's not what you or I learned in Sunday school or at home. Most of us grew up with the message: "Nice boys and girls do not lose their tempers!" What sense are we to make of Paul's words?

Well, to begin with, anger is a natural human emotion, a "feeling" if you will. And in and of themselves most emotions (most feelings) are *not sinful*.

"Be angry but do not sin," says Paul to the Ephesians and to us. It only makes things worse when preachers or parents say about any particular emotion, "You shouldn't feel that way." Feelings are feelings; you have them, and for the most part you can't control them. Saying "you shouldn't" increases frustration.

Indeed, *under certain controlled circumstances,* anger as a feeling can be helpful. Anger mobilizes us to defend ourselves from danger or to escape when defense is unwise or futile. Anger activates the so-called fight or flight mechanism within us. Anger, channeled properly, can be transformed into positive energy.

Years ago, I knew a middle school athlete whose anger at the drunk driver who caused his accident motivated him, day after day, to rehabilitate his crippled legs, motivated him through months of painful therapy to begin to walk again, and motivated him eventually to run and compete in high school sports.

Jesus himself may be a model of using anger constructively. While he warns in the Sermon on the Mount that anger can lead to murder, in John's Gospel, chapter 2, we find the familiar story of Jesus' rage at merchants selling cattle, sheep, and doves in the temple's inner court. You know the story. Jesus immediately made a whip of cords and drove them out, overturning their tables and sending them flying.

So, to sum up, anger is a natural emotion, dangerous to be sure, but an emotion that under certain circumstances can be channeled to good purposes.

Does this mean that it's okay to have a short fuse? That it's okay to throw tantrums? That it's okay to blow your top?

No. We have described anger *channeled and used constructively.* The Bible, however, does not excuse or condone anger that causes evil . . . (in the words of Ephesians) "that makes room for the Devil."

Listen to our text again:
   Be angry but do not sin;
   do not let the sun go down on your anger. . . .

Anger itself isn't sin. But when the sun goes down again and again on anger, when instead of "letting it go" anger is held tightly and nurtured, when anger turns to seething resentment and bitterness, the result is sin that harms both others and us.

So what are we to do? Paul sums up:
   Put away from you all bitterness and wrath and anger . . .
   and be kind to one another, tenderhearted, forgiving
   one another, as God in Christ has forgiven you.

As an anecdote to anger, Paul bids us forgive each other "as God in Christ has forgiven" us. But you know and I know that when you're angry at someone, forgiving that person isn't easy.

But notice—forgiveness begins with God, not with us. The good news is God's forgiveness of us. In Jesus Christ, God entered our world and drew near to his troubled people. In Jesus Christ, God nailed to the cross the world's anger and bitterness. In Jesus Christ, God took your sin and mine upon himself.

So, in Christ, you and I are able to forgive the targets of our anger, and ourselves, and thus let our anger go. We are able to give up our anger, not once and for all (that's probably not possible) but daily.

"Do not let the sun go down on your anger." This daily giving up of anger is possible because, in Christ, God has taken that anger upon himself.

So, when anger is a problem for you, end the day with a prayer like this: O God, this anger is making me a bitter person. As you have forgiven me, so enable me to forgive. As you have taken the world's anger upon yourself, so enable me to let mine go, that I may experience your gift of peace. Amen.

A Sermon on Fear

Context of the Sermon

The Reverend Adele Stiles Resmer, professor of homiletics at the Lutheran Theological Seminary at Philadelphia, preaches regularly in the seminary chapel. The immediate context for the sermon was a Reformation Day service with Holy Communion. The congregation was composed of students, professors, administration, staff, guests from the community, and visiting pastors. Approximately 100 people were there.

The sermon was preached about a month and a half after the tragedies of September 11, 2001. Students were expressing a desire to "get on with things," though they seemed to be overwhelmed by the fear that these events had generated. They were asking for some emotional distance from the events. The preacher tried to meet this pastoral need by helping them not only to see the events of September 11 in the broader context of their lives but also to begin to find reassurance in the promise of God's faithfulness.

Design and Development of the Sermon

Psalm 46 was a lectionary-appointed reading for the day. Its description of a tumultuous world in which the earth was changing, the mountains were shaking, and the waters roaring made it an especially appropriate text for the occasion. "Fear," as a designation of the human condition, became a natural refrain. "God is our refuge" became the antidote to fear, for it assures the listeners that "God is in the midst of the city" and that "he makes wars cease to the end of the earth."

The tone and movement of the psalm informs the tone and movement of the sermon. The rich imagery of Scripture encourages well-developed imagery in the proclamation. The sermon begins with daily fears that are a part of our lives, experiences that start early in life and continue into adulthood. The sermon then moves to the events of September 11 and attempts to broaden the interpretation of that tragedy, allowing it to remain a distinct experience while linking it with the general fears, large and small, that people live with day by day.

The refrain of the psalm, "God is our refuge" (refuge can also be translated "hiding place"), becomes a refrain in question form: "Where do you hide?" This refrain flows through the whole of the sermon, with minor variations, and helps the listener to move deeper into the question. The sermon turns to the language of promise, albeit not promise without cost. This is where Jesus Christ is named, woven into the imagery of the sermon and claimed as source of promise in his suffering and resurrection.

The focus sentence of the sermon is "God enfleshed in Jesus Christ is our hiding place that receives us and transforms us." The function sentence is "To assure listeners that God in Jesus is their source of safety and promise."

The Sermon:
"Where Do You Hide?"
(Based on Psalm 46)

Where do you hide?

You know when the terrors of the night
overpower your fatigued body
and you lie there with eyes wide open,
and ears primed for each muted sound
muscles tensed to respond to any movement
that could be a threat
large or small or not at all.

Where do you hide?

You know when the terrors of the day
crawl up your spine
before your feet ever hit the floor in the morning—
thoughts of the day and what it will require of you
sending you reeling,
your stomach lurching
as you hit the shower,
grab that first cup of coffee,
perhaps a few aspirin
to override any ache that may lie ahead.

Where do you hide?

It's okay to admit it—
It's not like you're alone here.
It may not be discussed in polite company
among adults anyway,
but the truth is
we all hide
in one place or another.

I suppose you could say
that we are a company of hiders.
Training begun in early childhood—
in the face of fun:
"hide and seek" in the backyard or street,
hiding behind a closed door with favorite book in hand.

And in the face of threat:
creeping away
from parental uproar,
even parental silence,
hiding with that favorite book
when friendships and inclusion
were longed for
but not to be found.

Training continued as adults:
hiding in socially valued ways more often than not—
work commitments that fill the calendar,
important, interesting and not so interesting, events;
hiding in ways that cannot be framed constructively—
excessive drinking, drugs, bingeing of one kind or another,
violence. . . .

Where do we hide, company of hiders?

Let it be said here:
September 11 may have done many horrendous things
in its day of terrorism,

senseless violence, death and loss,
but one thing it did not do—
it did not create the fear or the desire to hide
that runs through us individually and collectively
like the blood that travels through the matrix of arteries
and veins that lay below the surface of our skin.

It did not create our wide-eyed nights
or our jam-packed days
or our desire, perhaps even our need, to hide.

September 11 did put a larger than life
living and dying face
to the fears we carry around inside us.
It pulled off the skin
that covers those near-the-surface veins,
leaving our fears raw and exposed.
In the words of Psalm 46,
the mountains of the twin towers
not only shook in the midst of the sea of people,
buildings, and activity that are New York,
they roared and foamed
as those planes hit
and then collapsed into the earth,
changing the very earth itself.

Nation against nation
rising up against each other
like angry leviathans
rising up out of the deep
in cosmic-like battle.

Whatever kept us awake before,
whatever frightened and drove us before,
they are now writ large
and in full blazing color
grabbing hold of our fears
and running with them
as if on a flat-out marathon.

Now where do we hide, company of hiders?

Our usual hiding places will not stand
in the face of rising and falling seas,
of buildings collapsing,
the changing of the earth
as we saw on 9/11 and the days following,
in the rising of country against country,
and changes we have yet to imagine.

Events of this kind
cause our usual hiding places
to shake and wobble like meager lean-tos.
Some even collapse under the strain.

In the midst of all of this then
we hear the words of the psalmist:
"God is our refuge and strength;
a very present help in trouble.
Therefore we will not fear."
God alone is our hiding place, our refuge
God alone is the strength
that actually holds all of our fears
with tenderness and love
transforming them,
transforming us.

Corrie ten Boom lived in World War II Holland.
She and her extended family
were devout people,
as my grandmother would say.
They brought everything before God—
their fears for themselves,
their neighbors,
and the world as they knew it,
and as it was changing around them.

Conversation with God was woven
into the fabric of their day.

With fears placed repeatedly into the hands of God,
they became part of the underground in Holland,
providing a hiding place
along an escape route for Jewish people
who were at risk.

When I first read her book *The Hiding Place*,[1]
I thought it was about the hiding place
this family provided during the war.
I was wrong.

One hears the word "hiding place" only
after the family has been discovered
and sent to the local Gestapo headquarters
where Corrie shares her cell
with first one then other occupants—
mere ants.
After an initial, almost instinctive, desire to step on them,
she decides for company,
such that it is.
She leaves crumbs of her sparse bread,
which the ants regularly retrieve
and then disappear into a crack in the wall.
A day comes when shouts,
"Get ready to evacuate!" also come.
Corrie reaches quickly into her pillowcase,
throws out crumbs on the floor
for her cellmates.
None appear.
They remain hidden in the crack in the wall.

At that moment, Corrie got it:
She says, "I too have a hiding place when things are bad.
Jesus is this place,
The Rock cleft for me."[2]

God, in Jesus,
was the hiding place
where Corrie knew she could hide and be held safe.

Even in the face of prison cells, concentration camps,
and the death of beloved family members,
she knew her hiding place was Jesus.

In the prayer *"Anima Christi,"*
Spirit of Christ,
there is a petition,
"Within your wounds hide me."

The writer Ron Hansen reflects,
"We share with the human Jesus a host of vulnerabilities
to hurts and criticisms and temptations."
I'd add "fears" to that list.

He continues,
"And Jesus, having overcome them,
has become both our guide and refuge.
Hiding in his wounds is identical to
not hiding in ours."[3]

There's the transformation, my friends,
the transformation Corrie experienced,
the transformation that awaits us
as we turn to the hiding place that is God
clothed in the bruised and beaten,
resurrected body of Christ.
Hiding in those resurrected wounds,
find refuge,
find strength,
find a safe place
no matter how the earth be changed.

Hiding in the wounds of the resurrected Christ
we are with a God
who can be trusted to know our fears,
large as collapsing skyscrapers
and small as thoughts of exams in the dark night.

It is there
where our fears are so gently held by God

that we can say,
"Therefore we will not fear."

It is not that the world will be any less frightening.
The terrors of night and day
still go searching for places to alight
and burrow in.

Human capacity for destruction
and terror ride out ahead of us
into an unknown future.

Hidden in the wounds of Christ,
we are free,
free enough
to look and see and believe
the God
who is—
even as we gather here together—
working to bring an end to war,
breaking bows,
shattering spears,
receiving and transforming fears
so that we may share what we have,
even the crumbs out of a pillowcase
with those whom we normally would
squash under the heel of our shoe,
so that we may share with God in this work for peace.

Where do we hide, O company of hiders?

We hide in God
enfleshed in Jesus the Christ.
Though the earth be changed
and the waters rise up,
we will not fear,
for we have been transformed
we have been set free
by the holy hiding place itself. Amen.

A Sermon on Death

Context of the Sermon

The Reverend Robert Hughes preached this Easter-dawn sermon on April 4, 1999, to an ecumenical congregation assembled in the Music Pier on the boardwalk in Ocean City, New Jersey. The sunrise service is an annual event. It is supported by most of the Christian churches of the community, and typically it draws more than 400 worshipers.

Ordinarily, pastoral preaching occurs in the context of a clearly defined relationship between a pastor and a congregation in which the pastor has been "called." However, this sermon demonstrates that pastoral messages can be communicated between preachers and persons who are, for the most part, strangers to one another.

The sermon deals with the need to confront the reality of Jesus' death in order to experience the miracle of Jesus' resurrection. This message has pastoral and theological implications. In a culture in search of a self-constructed spirituality, it is important to affirm the biblical insight that faith is a gift of God to mourners.

Design and Development of the Sermon

The image of a disciplined military burial, which opens the sermon, serves several purposes. First, the order and dignity of a military burial provides a contrast to the hasty burial of the dead body of Jesus of Nazareth. Second, the realistic images evoked by both the Coppola film and the biblical account are intended to counter the superficial Easter theology of peeps from eggs and butterflies from cocoons. To persons who live in a death-denying culture, it is important to emphasize that Mary came to the garden not to view a resurrection but to anoint a corpse.

A second image, a flawed vision, is introduced in a humorous way but is employed to lead into the issue of crushed hopes and resulting despair. Jesus' followers expected a triumphant Messiah and were disappointed. Our generation seems hopelessly in search of a triumphant God. The risen Christ is the very one who was "crucified, dead, and buried." Faith in this Christ is awakened in us, not by scientific research, but by hearing and retelling the good news: "Christ is risen." "He is risen indeed." He can lead us out of despair into hope.

The focus sentence of the sermon is "The depth perception we call faith is given as a gift of God, through the Word, to persons with distorted vision." The function sentence is "[By the power of the Spirit,] to assist despairing listeners to experience the lively presence of the crucified and risen Christ."

The Sermon:
"The Gift of Corrected Vision"
(Based on John 20:15)

As the Francis Coppola film *Gardens of Stone* opens, the camera pans across row on row of white markers gleaming in the sunlight of Arlington National Cemetery. Then a familiar sound catches the ear, a military band playing "America the Beautiful." The camera moves closer. We see a flag-draped coffin borne from the cemetery chapel by soldiers in tailored uniforms. The burial detail moves with precision to hushed commands. Gloved hands lift the coffin onto a horse-drawn wagon, and the procession moves off toward the gravesite. A chaplain speaks words familiar to most of us. A flag, precisely folded by two soldiers, is presented to a spouse who has tear-stained eyes. "On behalf of the President of the United States, please accept this . . . in recognition of your loved one's faithful service." Three volleys are fired, taps are played, and it's over.

Contrast this picture of dignified solemnity with another burial. It is late on a Friday afternoon, just prior to sunset and the beginning of the Jewish Sabbath. Two disciples are lugging Jesus' body into a garden. One disciple has wrapped his arms around Jesus' torso from behind. The other is carrying him by his legs. Joseph of Arimathea and Nicodemus struggle under the weight as they haul the body of their friend into a hollow rock tomb. This is how the German expressionist Emil Nolde pictures the burial of Jesus in his painting *The Entombment*.[4]

We know from chapter 19 of the Gospel of John that when the friends had laid the lifeless Jesus in the tomb, probably on a rock shelf, they anointed the body with spices, wrapped it in linen, and sealed the tomb—as they believed—forever. At the burial of Jesus of Nazareth, there was no band or honor guard smartly attired. No chaplain was present to say the correct words. No firing squad raised rifles for a ceremonial volley.

"Crucified, dead, and buried."
Four little words, yet they speak volumes.
"Crucified, dead, and buried."
The meaning is clear—a living Jesus had become a corpse.

Jesus said to (Mary), "Woman, why are you weeping? Whom are you looking for?" Did tears blind the eyes of Mary Magdalene when she hurried to the garden tomb on the first Easter morning? The garden—the whole world—was still in darkness and Mary could see only that the stone had been taken away. Mary's depth perception was flawed. She drew the simplest and most direct inference from visual evidence—the body of Jesus had been stolen. That was the anguished message Mary carried back to Peter and "the other disciple." "They have taken the Lord out of the tomb, and we do not know where they have laid him."

Fifteen years ago, when my eyes and I turned forty-six, I first became aware that my near vision was getting cloudy. A crisis was upon me. My arms, always short, could no longer be extended to read menus in dimly lit restaurants. Reading in public became a guessing game. The optometrist said, "No problem! The left eye remains 20–20, so we can correct the weak eye for close work. A single contact lens will do."

And it did, except that with one contact lens and one uncorrected eye, though I could see clearly, I did lose my depth perception. Going up and down the steps became an adventure. Instead of merely stumbling in dark hallways, I was lurching like a drunken person outdoors—in daylight. Friends made discreet inquiries about the state of my health. My lawn, never a work of art, resembled an experiment in contour plowing. Yes, depth perception is critical to accurate sight.

"Woman, why are you weeping? For whom are you looking?"

For Mary and for Jesus' other disciples faulty depth perception led to despair. And is it any wonder? The disciples had followed Jesus to Jerusalem expecting to help him claim a kingdom, expecting positions of responsibility in the new administration, expecting to be somebody for the first time in their lives.

Instead, in Gethsemane they watched their Lord betrayed by soldiers. At least in John's account, two disciples saw him led from the house of Caiaphas to Pilate's headquarters. Some stood by as Pilate washed his hands of Jesus. On Golgotha the three Marys and John huddled by the cross of Christ while the others watched from a safe distance. The disciples' hopes ended on that hill. Their leader was dead, and now even his body was gone. On the surface it must have seemed like a hideous dream.

"Why are you weeping? For whom are you looking?" I believe that many today can relate to Mary's dilemma. Can you? A whole generation, blinded by watery eyes, seems to be waiting for something to startle them into faith. Are you such a one?

Perhaps the church has failed in its proclamation. Perhaps ordinary Christians have neglected to share the story of the risen Christ with sufficient clarity and commitment. Perhaps the lives of believers seem so devoid of spiritual vitality that it is difficult for anyone to believe that Christ is alive. Perhaps!

But there is another explanation. *Corpse* is not a pleasant word to say or to think about. Most of us do not come to grips easily with the icy fingers of death.

And yet I used the word *corpse* earlier and I repeat it now for shock value, a shock similar to the jolt when a wet finger touches a bare wire. Because until you and I grasp the plain meaning of *corpse*, of "crucified, dead, and buried," we will be incapable of comprehending the miracle of a second creedal affirmation.

"On the third day [Jesus] rose from the dead." The corpse of the person who was Jesus was raised to new life by the power of

God. Can you and I ever grasp the significance of such an event? How does faith in this miracle of God come to life in us? There are clues in our text. We do know that, even with flawed vision, at least two disciples did not sit around whining about their bleak situation. When Mary came running to Peter and "the other disciple" with the message, "They have taken the Lord out of the tomb, and we do not know where they have laid him," Peter and a nameless disciple ran as fast as they could to see for themselves. What they saw was what Mary saw, an empty tomb with linen wrapping rolled up neatly. But unlike Mary before them, these two at least put themselves in position to have their vision corrected.

Of the two, Peter had a scientific bent. Peter inspected the grave clothes. Peter examined the evidence, although the Bible never states that Peter believed. Rather, the nameless disciple who entered the tomb last, the one who saw little by way of evidence, "saw" the most by faith.

Like Peter, the scientific minds of this generation would wish to examine the evidence, to put the linen under powerful microscopes, to take DNA samples if possible. Most of us, if it were available, would like irrefutable proof. Was Jesus' body carried away by grave robbers? Or did the soldiers desecrate the body? Or did Jesus, in fact, rise from the dead?

Sorry! Such proof is not available to us. You and I live on the faith side of Easter day. Jesus will not meet you or me in the half-light of Joseph's garden. He will not come striding into this room displaying scarred hands for examination. Nor are we likely to hear our names spoken aloud by him.

But listen! There is good news for us. As Mary hurried to tell the disciples, "I have seen the Lord," and as we gather to retell the wondrous stories of Jesus, the one who was a corpse comes into our midst, into our lives, and we do believe.

The depth perception we call faith is given to us as a gift of God. And such moments of clear vision come—whether the gathering is in a seaside pavilion at first light, or in an earthen basement in Kosovo, with artillery fire punctuating the dawn, or in the simplicity of a local parish church. Our tears and doubts, our quarrels and confusion, our grief and denial are crucified and buried with Jesus. And risen with him, as from the grave itself, are the forgiveness of sins, salvation, and eternal life.

Indeed, there is more in life than meets the uncorrected eye! "Christ is risen. He is risen indeed. Alleluia!" Amen.

Conclusion

We have affirmed that what makes preaching pastoral, apart from the theological and pastoral content of individual sermons, is the cumulative impact of those sermons on listeners. The clergy leader who is determined to be pastoral in and through preaching is confronted with questions. Are my sermons helping to heal hurts in the lives of my congregants? Are my sermons effective as conduits of God's comfort?

While the impact on listeners of any given sermon is nearly impossible to measure, the objectives detailed in chapter 4, if kept firmly in mind during preparation, will assist preachers to become more effective and helpful communicators. Does the sermon

- give voice to human lament?
- assist listeners to face the reality of one aspect of suffering?
- make suffering endurable by communicating the love and concern of God and the Christian community?
- strengthen faith in God?
- give a sense of joy in the midst of trouble?

No single sermon can relate fully the good news of the gospel to what the troubled parishioner is experiencing. No single sermon can "make the wounded whole." Yet in an extended relationship between pastor and people, which includes the type of preaching we have advocated, the love of Jesus can "heal the sin-sick soul."

We dedicate this book to those who seek faithfully to bring God's healing balm to suffering believers.

Notes

Preface

1. J. Randal Nichols, *The Restoring Word: Preaching as Pastoral Communication* (San Francisco: Harper & Row, 1987).

2. Lloyd M. Perry and Charles M. Sell, *Speaking to Life's Problems: A Sourcebook for Preaching and Teaching* (Chicago: Moody Press, 1983).

3. Donald Capps, *Pastoral Counseling and Preaching: A Quest for an Integrated Ministry* (Philadelphia: Westminster, 1980).

4. Robert G. Hughes and Robert Kysar, *Preaching Doctrine for the Twenty-First Century* (Minneapolis: Fortress Press, 1997).

5. Erhard S. Gerstenberger and Wolfgang Schrage, *Suffering*, trans. John E. Steely (Nashville: Abingdon, 1977).

1. The Pain of Suffering

1. Douglas John Hall, *God and Human Suffering: An Exercise in the Theology of the Cross* (Minneapolis: Augsburg, 1986), 38.

2. Ibid., 45.

3. See J. Christiaan Beker, *Suffering and Hope* (Philadelphia: Fortress Press, 1987), chap. 2, for the Old Testament belief in punishment and rewards, its source and its advantages.

4. William B. Ward, *Out of the Whirlwind: Answers to the Problem of Suffering from the Book of Job* (Richmond: John Knox, 1958), 40.

5. Harold S. Kushner, *When Bad Things Happen to Good People* (New York: Schocken, 1981), 2.

6. Ibid., 10.

7. Ibid., 24–26.

8. Erhard S. Gerstenberger and Wolfgang Schrage, *Suffering*, trans. John Steely (Nashville: Abingdon, 1977), 215–16.

9. See Dorothee Soelle, *Suffering,* trans. Everett R. Kalin (Philadelphia: Fortress Press, 1975), 110–11.

10. Kushner, *When Bad Things Happen,* 19.

11. Walter von Loewenich, *Luther's Theology of the Cross,* trans. Herbert J. A. Bouman (Minneapolis: Augsburg, 1976), 28.

12. Ibid., 119.

13. Carl R. Rogers, ed., *The Therapeutic Relationship and Its Impact* (Madison: Univ. of Wisconsin Press, 1967), 104–6.

2. The Believer's Struggle with Suffering

1. Thornton Wilder, *The Bridge of San Luis Rey* (New York: Boni, 1928), 23.

2. Foster R. McCurley and Alan G. Weitzman, *Making Sense Out of Sorrow: A Journey of Faith* (Valley Forge, Pa.: Trinity Press International, 1995), 15.

3. C. S. Lewis, *A Grief Observed* (New York: Seabury, 1963), 4–5.

4. Robert G. Hughes, *A Trumpet in Darkness: Preaching to Mourners* (Mifflintown, Pa.: Sigler, 1997), 62–63.

5. *Luther's Works,* vol. 31 (Philadelphia: Fortress Press, 1957), 40.

6. Douglas John Hall, *God and Human Suffering: An Exercise in the Theology of the Cross* (Minneapolis: Augsburg, 1986), 15.

7. David G. Buttrick, *The Mystery and the Passion: A Homiletic Reading of the Gospel* (Minneapolis: Fortress Press, 1986), 98.

8. Thomas Long, *The Witness of Preaching* (Louisville: Westminster John Knox, 1989), 34.

9. Douglas John Hall, *Lighten Our Darkness: Toward an Indigenous Theology of the Cross* (Philadelphia: Westminster, 1976), 113–14.

10. John Baillie, *The Idea of Revelation in Recent Thought* (New York: Columbia Univ. Press, 1956), 32.

11. Howard W. Stone, *Crisis Counseling* (Philadelphia: Fortress Press, 1976), 22.

3. The Church's Attempt to Address Suffering

1. Harry Emerson Fosdick, "What Is the Matter with Preaching?" *Harper's Magazine* (July 1928); reprinted in Lionel Crocker, ed., *Harry Emerson Fosdick's Art of Preaching: An Anthology* (Springfield, Ill.: Charles C. Thomas, 1971), chap. 2.

2. Crocker, *Fosdick's Art of Preaching,* 29.

3. Ibid., 34.

4. Ibid., 31.

5. Ibid.

6. Harry Emerson Fosdick, "Personal Counseling and Preaching," *Pastoral Psychology* 3.22 (March 1952); reprinted in Crocker, *Fosdick's Art of Preaching*, 55.

7. Harry Emerson Fosdick, *The Living of These Days* (New York: Harper & Row, 1956), 100.

8. From Fosdick, "What Is the Matter with Preaching?"

9. For this history in detail, see Donald Meyer, *The Positive Thinkers* (New York: Doubleday, 1965).

10. More information regarding the roots of positive thinking and an indictment of the movement can be found in "The Positive Thinking Preachers: A Critique," an article by Robert Hughes, *Academy Accents: The Newsletter of the Academy of Preachers* 4.2 (May 1988).

11. Clyde E. Fant Jr. and William M. Pinson Jr., *Twenty Centuries of Great Preaching*, vol. 11 (Waco, Tex.: Word, 1971), 226.

12. Jackson W. Carroll, "Robert H. Schuller," in *Concise Encyclopedia of Preaching*, ed. William H. Willimon and Richard Lischer (Louisville: Westminster John Knox, 1995), 430.

13. Robert H. Schuller, "Turn Your Scars into Stars!" *The Twentieth Century Pulpit*, vol. 2, ed. James Cox (Nashville: Abingdon, 1981), 178.

14. Carroll, "Robert H. Schuller," 432.

15. Douglas John Hall, *God and Human Suffering: An Exercise in the Theology of the Cross* (Minneapolis: Augsburg, 1986), 21.

16. Schuller, "Turn Your Scars into Stars!" 178.

17. Jeffrey Hadden and Charles Swann, *Prime Time Preachers: The Rising Power of Televangelism* (New York: Addison-Wesley, 1981), 32.

18. Lloyd M. Perry and Charles M. Sell, *Speaking to Life's Problems: A Sourcebook for Preaching and Teaching* (Chicago: Moody Press, 1983), 33.

19. Carroll, "Robert H. Schuller," 361.

20. Donald Capps, *Pastoral Counseling and Preaching: A Quest for an Integrated Ministry* (Philadelphia: Westminster, 1980).

21. Ibid., 11.

22. Ibid., 45.

23. Ibid., 47.

24. Ibid., 51.

25. J. Randall Nichols, *The Restoring Word: Preaching as Pastoral Communication* (New York: Harper & Row, 1987), 4.

26. Ibid., 18.

27. Ibid., 17–18.

28. Ibid., 67.

29. Ibid., 90.

30. Ibid., 128.

31. Ibid., 150.

4. The Pastoral Response to Suffering

1. Robert G. Hughes, *A Trumpet in Darkness: Preaching to Mourners* (Mifflintown, Pa.: Sigler, 1997), 16.

2. Most of this section was first published in Aden's article, "Reflections on Pastoral Preaching," *Parish Practice Notebook* 38 (Fall 1992) (Philadelphia: Lutheran Theological Seminary, 1992), 1–3.

3. Lloyd M. Perry and Charles M. Sell, *Speaking to Life's Problems: A Sourcebook for Preaching and Teaching* (Chicago: Moody Press, 1983), 26.

4. *Luther: Letters of Spiritual Counsel,* ed. and trans. Theodore G. Tappert (Philadelphia: Westminster, 1945), 96.

5. Donald Capps, *Reframing: A New Method in Pastoral Care* (Minneapolis: Fortress Press, 1990).

6. Paul Tillich, *Systematic Theology,* vol. 1 (Chicago: Univ. of Chicago Press, 1951), 3.

7. J. Randall Nichols, *The Restoring Word: Preaching as Pastoral Communication* (New York: Harper & Row, 1987), 13.

8. Ibid., 15.

9. Douglas John Hall, *Lighten Our Darkness* (Philadelphia: Westminster, 1976), 221.

10. This sermon, preached by Hughes at Zion Lutheran Church, Philadelphia, on the Third Sunday of Easter 2001, displays many of the characteristics of pastoral preaching about suffering and is quoted at length.

5. Preaching to Believers Who Experience Loss

1. C. S. Lewis, *A Grief Observed* (New York: Seabury, 1963); and Nicholas Wolterstorff, *Lament for a Son* (Grand Rapids: Eerdmans, 1987).

2. Wolterstorff, *Lament for a Son,* 24.

3. Ibid., 9.

4. Ibid., 15.

5. Ibid., 19.

6. Ibid., 17.

7. Ibid. 28.

8. Ibid., 33.

9. Ibid., 46.

10. Ibid., 47.

11. Ibid., 55.

12. Ibid., 71.

13. Ibid., 56.

14. Ibid., 57.

15. Ibid., 36.

16. Ibid., 31.

17. Ibid.

18. Ibid., 34.

19. Ibid.

20. Ibid., 68.

21. Ibid.

22. Ibid., 67.

23. Ibid., 69.

24. Ibid., 90.

25. Ibid., 91.

26. Ibid., 101.

27. Ibid.

28. Ibid.

29. Ibid., 34.

30. For a discussion of the dynamics of various kinds of death, see Robert G. Hughes, *A Trumpet in Darkness: Preaching to Mourners* (Mifflintown, Pa.: Sigler, 1997), 24–47.

31. Nelson DeMille, *The Gold Coast* (New York: Warner, 1990), 374.

32. *Lutheran Book of Worship:* Ministers Desk Edition (Minneapolis: Augsburg; Philadelphia: Board of Publication, Lutheran Church in America, 1978), 336.

33. DeMille, *Gold Coast,* 31.

34. Lloyd R. Bailey Sr., *Biblical Perspectives on Death* (Philadelphia: Fortress Press, 1979).

35. *Lutheran Book of Worship,* 311.

6. Preaching to Believers Who Are Ill

1. Sherwin B. Nuland, *How We Die: Reflections on Life's Final Chapter* (New York: Vintage, 1995), 65–66.

2. Paul Tillich, *The Courage to Be* (New Haven, Conn.: Yale Univ. Press, 1952), 39.

3. Ibid., 42–54.

4. Nuland, *How We Die,* 65–66.

5. Fred B. Craddock, *Overhearing the Gospel* (Nashville: Abingdon, 1987), 104.

6. Ibid., 112.

7. Eudora Welty, *One Writer's Beginnings* (New York: Warner, 1983), 92.

8. *Dead Poets Society*, a novel by N. H. Kleinbaum, based on the motion picture written by Tom Schulman (New York: Bantam, 1989), 60.

9. Ibid., 60.

10. John Updike, *Rabbit at Rest* (New York: Fawcett Columbine, 1990), 1.

11. Ibid., 4.

12. Ibid., 5.

13. Ibid., 6–7.

14. Ibid.

15. Tillich, *Courage to Be.*

16. Viktor E. Frankl, *From Death-Camp to Existentialism* (Boston: Beacon, 1959), 76.

17. Morton T. Kelsey, *Healing and Christianity* (New York: Harper & Row, 1973), 54.

18. Robert Kysar, *Called to Care: Biblical Images for Social Ministry* (Minneapolis: Fortress Press, 1991), 32.

19. Fred Craddock, *Preaching* (Nashville: Abingdon, 1985), 97.

20. Reginald H. Fuller, *Preaching the New Lectionary: The Word of God for the Church Today* (Collegeville, Minn.: Liturgical, 1971), 159.

21. "Service of the Word for Healing," *Occasional Services* (Minneapolis: Augsburg; Philadelphia: Board of Publication, Lutheran Church in America, 1982), 91.

22. Wayne E. Oates, *Pastoral Care and Counseling in Grief and Separation* (Philadelphia: Fortress Press, 1976).

7. Preaching to Believers Who Experience Violence

1. Rollo May, *Power and Innocence: A Search for the Sources of Violence* (New York: Norton, 1972).

2. Ibid., 82.

3. Ibid., 83.

4. Ibid.

5. Ibid., 84.

6. Ibid.

7. Paul Tillich, *Love, Power, and Justice* (New York: Oxford Univ. Press, 1954), 85.

8. May, *Power and Innocence*, 92.

9. W. Somerset Maugham, *Of Human Bondage* (Garden City, N.Y.: International Collectors Library, 1936).

10. Ibid., 43.

11. May, *Power and Innocence*, 42.

12. Ibid., 86.

13. Ibid.

14. Ibid., 87.

15. Ibid.

16. Ibid., 88.

17. Jürgen Moltmann, *The Crucified God* (New York: Harper & Row, 1974), 293.

18. C. S. Lewis, *A Grief Observed* (New York: Seabury, 1963), 38.

19. Dorothee Soelle, *Suffering*, trans. Everett Kalin (Philadelphia: Fortress Press, 1975), 70–75.

20. Ibid., 85.

21. The story of the woman has parallels in the narrative of the anointing at Bethany (Mark 14:3-9; cf. Matt. 26:6-13 and John 12:1-8). However, the focus of the Bethany account is Jesus' anointing for burial, whereas Luke's treatment centers on the woman, hospitality issues, and Jesus' announcement of her forgiveness.

22. *Lutheran Book of Worship* (Minneapolis: Augsburg; Philadelphia: Board of Publication, Lutheran Church in America, 1978), 56.

23. Ibid.

24. *The Twentieth Century Pulpit*, vol. 2, ed. James W. Cox (Nashville: Abingdon, 1981), 48–49.

25. Pat Conroy, *The Prince of Tides* (New York: Bantam, 1987), 442–43.

8. Preaching to Believers Who Are Fearful

1. Rollo May, *The Meaning of Anxiety* (New York: Ronald, 1950), 191.

2. Quoted in ibid., 62.

3. *The Interpreter's Dictionary of the Bible*, vol. 2 (Nashville: Abingdon, 1962), 258.

4. Edgar N. Jackson, *A Psychology for Preaching* (Great Neck, N.Y.: Channel, 1961), 85.

5. Ibid., 94.

6. The narrative is retold here from memory, and thus it may differ in details from John's own account.

7. See also Psalm 46, which assures us of the presence of God, our refuge and strength, in the midst of calamity.

8. Flannery O'Connor, *The Complete Stories* (New York: Farrar, Straus, and Giroux, 1986), 3–14.

9. Ibid., 14.

10. Tom Ferrick Jr. in the *Philadelphia Inquirer* (Sept. 12, 2001), A5.

11. Ernest Campbell, *Locked in a Room with Open Doors* (Waco, Tex.: Word, 1976).

12. *Lutheran Book of Worship* (Minneapolis: Augsburg; Philadelphia: Board of Publication, Lutheran Church in America, 1978), 320.

13. Michael Crawford, "On Eagle's Wings," recorded on a CD by the same name (Atlantic Recording Corporation, 1998).

14. *With One Voice* (Minneapolis: Augsburg Fortress, 1995), hymn 779.

15. Ibid., hymn 780.

9. Preaching to Believers Who Experience Failure

1. Arthur Miller, *Death of a Salesman* (New York: Viking, 1949).

2. Ibid., 31.

3. Ibid., 62.

4. Ibid., 36.

5. Ibid., 82.

6. Quoted in Douglas John Hall, *God and Human Suffering* (Minneapolis: Augsburg, 1986), 41.

7. Ibid., 52.

8. Karen Horney, *Neurosis and Human Growth: The Struggle toward Self-Realization* (New York: Norton, 1950). A summary of Horney's theory is also found in LeRoy Aden and David G. Benner, eds., *Counseling and the Human Predicament: A Study of Sin, Guilt, and Forgiveness* (Grand Rapids: Baker, 1989), 150ff.

9. Ibid., 18.

10. Horney defines the real self as "the 'original' force toward individual growth and fulfillment." Later she defines it as "the spring of emotional forces, of constructive energies, of directive and judiciary powers" (ibid., 157, 173).

11. Ibid., 68.

12. Ibid., 64.

13. Miller, *Death of a Salesman*, 35.

14. Ibid., 36.

15. Ibid., 64.

16. Ibid., 67.

17. Ibid., 132–33.

18. Helen Merrell Lynd, *On Shame and the Search for Identity* (New York: Science Editions, 1962), 49.

19. Ibid., 50.

20. Miller, *Death of a Salesman*, 35.

21. Ibid., 35.

22. Ibid.

23. Ibid., 123.

24. Ibid., 124.

25. Ibid.

26. Ibid., 138.

27. Frederick Buechner, *The Alphabet of Grace* (New York: Seabury, 1970), 25.

28. Miller, *Death of a Salesman*, 104.

29. Ibid., 139.

30. Robert Frost, "On a Tree Fallen across the Road," in *The Poetry of Robert Frost*, ed. Edward Connory Latham (New York: Henry Holt, 1969), 238. Used by permission.

31. Jürgen Moltmann, *The Crucified God* (New York: Harper and Row, 1974), 276.

32. Thomas Long, "Homiletical Notes for Eastertide," *Journal for Preachers* (Easter 1985): 4.

33. Fred B. Craddock, *John* (Atlanta: John Knox, 1982), 142.

10. Samples of Pastoral Preaching

1. Corrie ten Boom, with John and Elizabeth Sherrill, *The Hiding Place* (Washington Depot, Conn.: Chosen, 1971).

3. Ibid., 155–56.

3. Ron Hansen, *A Stay against Confusion: Essays on Faith and Fiction* (New York: HarperCollins, 2001), 171.

4. This description of Jesus' burial from the Nolde painting is found in Thomas H. Troeger, *Creating Fresh Images for Preaching: New Rungs for Jacob's Ladder* (Valley Forge, Pa.: Judson, 1982), 15.

Index of Names and Subjects

Index of Biblical References